The Internet and Us

Editor: Tracy Biram

Volume 371

Independence Educational Publishers

First published by Independence Educational Publishers

The Studio, High Green

Great Shelford

Cambridge CB22 5EG

England

© Independence 2020

ISBN-13: 978 1 86168 828 6

Printed in Great Britain

Zenith Print Group

Contents

Introduction

The Internet and Us is Volume 371 in the **ISSUES** series. The aim of the series is to offer current, diverse information about important issues in our world, from a UK perspective.

ABOUT THE INTERNET AND US

In the UK we spend approximately 50 days a year online. As the internet is an increasingly important part of our lives, we must ask ourselves: 'how does the internet affect me?'. This book explores the role the internet plays, and how we can stay safe online.

OUR SOURCES

Titles in the **ISSUES** series are designed to function as educational resource books, providing a balanced overview of a specific subject.

The information in our books is comprised of facts, articles and opinions from many different sources, including:

♦ Newspaper reports and opinion pieces

♦ Website factsheets

♦ Magazine and journal articles

♦ Statistics and surveys

♦ Government reports

♦ Literature from special interest groups.

A NOTE ON CRITICAL EVALUATION

Because the information reprinted here is from a number of different sources, readers should bear in mind the origin of the text and whether the source is likely to have a particular bias when presenting information (or when conducting their research). It is hoped that, as you read about the many aspects of the issues explored in this book, you will critically evaluate the information presented.

It is important that you decide whether you are being presented with facts or opinions. Does the writer give a biased or unbiased report? If an opinion is being expressed, do you agree with the writer? Is there potential bias to the 'facts' or statistics behind an article?

ASSIGNMENTS

In the back of this book, you will find a selection of assignments designed to help you engage with the articles you have been reading and to explore your own opinions. Some tasks will take longer than others and there is a mixture of design, writing and research-based activities that you can complete alone or in a group.

FURTHER RESEARCH

At the end of each article we have listed its source and a website that you can visit if you would like to conduct your own research. Please remember to critically evaluate any sources that you consult and consider whether the information you are viewing is accurate and unbiased.

Useful Websites

www.blogs.coventry.ac.uk

www.blogs.lse.ac.uk

www.childnet.com

www.childrenscommissioner.gov.uk

www.femalefirst.co.uk

www.independent.co.uk

www.inews.co.uk

www.kaspersky.co.uk

www.life.spectator.co.uk

www.ofcom.org.uk

www.ons.gov.uk

www.ox.ac.uk

www.shoutoutuk.org

www.telegraph.co.uk

www.theconversation.com

www.thinkuknow.co.uk

www.whatmobile.net

www.yougov.co.uk

www.young.scot

www.youthemployment.org.uk

Internet access

Internet access in Great Britain, including how many people have the internet, how they access it and what they use it for.

By Cecil Prescott

Main points

♦ 87% of all adults used the internet daily or almost every day in 2019.

♦ In 2019, 61% of households without the internet did not feel that they needed the internet.

♦ In 2019, for the first time, more than half of adults aged 65 years and over shopped online, at 54%.

♦ The percentage of adults who make video or voice calls over the internet has more than trebled over the past decade, to 50% in 2019.

♦ In 2019, 7% of adults suffered fraudulent debit or credit card use from using the internet in the last 12 months.

9 in 10 adults use the internet at least weekly

Of all adults, 87% used the internet daily in 2019, with an additional 4% of adults using it at least weekly but not daily.

While there was only a 2 percentage point increase in daily use since 2018, it has risen by 32 percentage points in the last decade.

While almost all adults aged 16 to 44 years used the internet daily or almost every day (99%), the older age groups used it less frequently. This reduced across the older age groups, as 61% of adults aged 65 years and over used the internet daily, while 24% had not used the internet in the last three months (Figure 2).

Over 8 out of 10 adults access the internet 'on the go'

Among all adults, 84% had used the internet 'on the go' in 2019, using a mobile phone, smartphone, laptop, tablet or handheld device (Figure 3).

In 2019, the most common type of device used to access the internet on the go was a mobile phone or smartphone at

Figure 2: There are still many adults aged 55 years and over who have not used the internet in the last three months

Internet use within the last three months, Great Britain, 2019

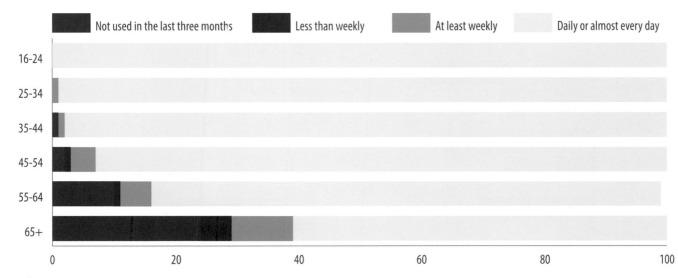

Source: Office for National Statistics – Opinions and Lifestyle Survey

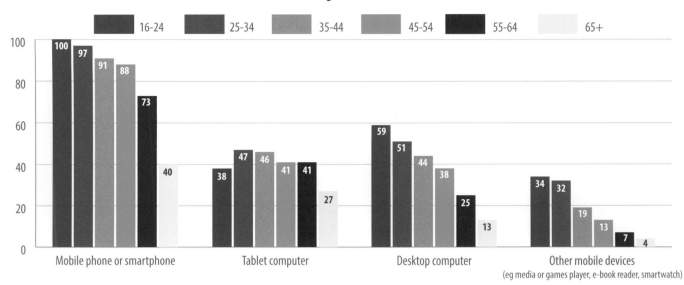

Figure 3: Mobile phones and smartphones are by far the most popular devices to access the internet on the go

Devices used to access the internet on the go within the last three months, Great Britain, 2019

Source: Office for National Statistics – Opinions and Lifestyle Survey

79%. This has risen by 26 percentage points since 2013, from 53%. Other mobile devices were used far less to access the internet on the go, with 39% of adults using a tablet and 36% of adults using a laptop.

Email remains the most common internet activity

Email was used by 86% of adults in 2019, more than any other internet activity. Other widely used activities included finding information about goods or services (78%), internet

Figure 4: Other internet activities have been catching up with sending emails over the last decade

Internet activities within the last three months, Great Britain, 2009 and 2019

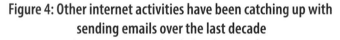

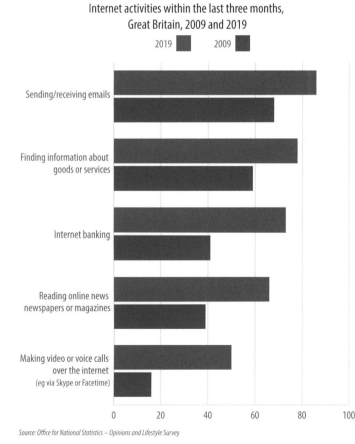

Source: Office for National Statistics – Opinions and Lifestyle Survey

banking (73%) and use of instant messaging services such as Skype and WhatsApp (72%).

There has broadly been growth in the percentage of adults who perform internet activities. Adults looking for health-related information grew from 54% in 2018 to 63% in 2019, while adults listening to music grew to 65% in 2019, up from 58% in 2018. The only activity measured that showed a decrease was uploading created content to a website to be shared, which dropped to 35% of adults in 2019, down from 48% in 2017 when it was last measured.

There were some differences in the activities that men and women carried out over the internet, with a higher percentage of women using it for social networking, compared with men (71% and 64% respectively). Furthermore, 68% of women looked for health-related information online, compared with 59% of men. However, the proportion of men who sold goods or services over the internet was 10 percentage points higher than women, at 34% and 24% respectively.

The percentage of adults making voice or video calls using the internet more than trebled over the past decade, rising from 16% in 2009, to 50% in 2019. With high street bank closures continuing to rise, internet banking has also shown a large percentage point increase, rising by 32 percentage points since 2009 (Figure 4).

12 August 2019

New survey finds majority of internet users have a positive experience online, but potential for digital divide to widen

Research from the Oxford Internet Institute (OII), part of the University of Oxford, has revealed a rapid increase in use of the internet for commercial, banking and entertainment purposes.

The number of people paying bills online, watching films and TV series' and streaming music via the internet has increased significantly since 2013.

However, there is a growing divide in experience and perception between those who use the internet and those who do not, which could lead to non-users potentially missing out on access to key services, widening the 'digital divide'.

The findings of the 2019 Oxford Internet Survey (OxIS) show that while harmful experiences on the internet like viruses or theft of credit card details have not increased, 72% of non-internet users believe the internet threatens privacy, compared to 52% of those who actually use the internet.

Internet users are also far more likely to believe 'technology makes things better' - 79% of users agree with that sentiment, compared to just 29% of non-users.

Dr Grant Blank, Survey Research Fellow, Oxford Internet Institute, and author of the survey, said:

'The majority of people are having positive experiences of internet use, regularly going online to watch their favourite shows or pay their utility bills.

'However there is a widening perception gap between internet users and non-users, with non-users resolutely avoiding the internet. Often these non-users are from low income groups, where being online could potentially improve their quality of life.

'There's an interesting paradox here with internet users being less likely to take action to protect their privacy while non-users tend to be put off by privacy concerns. These concerns could perpetuate the digital divide, with many people missing out on the benefits of the internet, such as access to health information, employment opportunities and reduced prices online.

'There is a real opportunity to engage with non-users to address their concerns and help them understand the opportunities the internet can bring. We hope this survey contributes to the public debate about what further steps can be taken to narrow the digital divide.'

The Oxford Internet Survey 2019 is sponsored by the Department for Digital, Culture, Media and Sport (DCMS), BT and Google.

Minister for Digital Matt Warman MP said:

'It is great to see an increasing number of people are reaping the huge benefits of being online. From paying bills, streaming their favourite songs to connecting with friends and family across the globe.

'To help more people get online we launched our £400,000 Digital Inclusion Fund to help older and disabled people get online and acquire new digital skills. Through our Digital Skills Partnership we are continuing to work with our partners across the public, private and charity sectors to boost people's capability and confidence in a collaborative way so everyone can benefit from our world-leading digital economy.'

Andy Wales, Chief Digital Impact and Sustainability Officer, BT said:

'Helping motivate people who lack confidence to get online is essential to bridge the digital divide. BT is passionate about building people's digital skills and helping them to navigate new technologies to improve their lives and drive better productivity for the UK economy.'

Commercial and leisure use of the internet

◆ Almost all forms of online commercial activity have increased sharply in the last six years, with a significant rise in the number of people using the internet to pay bills. 83% of internet users now pay their bills online, up from 59% in 2013.

◆ 72% of internet users watch films and series on platforms such as Netflix and Amazon Prime, up from just 49% in 2013.

◆ People are increasingly going online to follow their favourite celebrities, with 66% of users in 2019 using platforms such as Instagram and Twitter to do so, up from 44% in 2013.

◆ Listening to music online has increased, with 76% of users now using channels such as Spotify and YouTube to stream their favourite songs, compared to 64% in 2013.

Reasons for not being online

◆ Among non-internet users 69% cite 'lack of interest' as the main reason for not being online, down from 82% in 2013.

◆ 18% of non-users cite a lack of knowledge as a reason not to go online, with 10% expressing privacy concerns.

◆ Financial barriers are another reason for not accessing the internet; 40% of non-users report annual incomes below £12,500.

Internet risks declining

◆ Internet users believe the risks of internet use are stable or declining, with 52% of users reporting concerns about computer malware and viruses in 2019, compared to 69% in 2013.

◆ The number of people receiving malware or viruses has decreased since 2013, down from 30% in 2013 to 12% in 2019. Alongside this, the proportion of respondents taking steps to protect themselves against malware or a virus has fallen dramatically, down from 76% in 2013 to just 33% in 2019.

User-created content online

◆ The use of the internet for various forms of content production has been much more stable in the last six years. Posting on social media remains the most popular form of content production, up 8 percentage points to 79% of internet users in 2019.

◆ Other activities such as selling products online remain stable at just over 40% of internet users.

◆ Maintaining a personal website is up 5 percentage points at 23% and posting your own pictures is up 6 percentage points at 69% respectively.

◆ Writing a blog has declined by 6 percentage points at 14% of internet users in 2019, perhaps reflecting the emergence of 'threads' and the option to write longer posts and notes on platforms such as Facebook and Twitter.

Attitudes to online advertising

◆ New for 2019, the survey also examined whether people were comfortable with targeted online advertisements. Some 68% of all people surveyed, including users and non-users, dislike the use of targeted advertising and the use of tracking data for commercial purposes.

9 September 2019

UK's screen time stats revealed

Survey reveals UK adults spend around 50 days a year on their mobiles.

A new study into people's screen time and attitudes towards their mobile devices has revealed:

♦ 37 per cent of people currently track their smartphone screen time. This rose to almost 60 per cent in 16 to 25-year-olds.

♦ 15 per cent of the respondents says they spend more than six hours every day on a mobile device!

♦ The UK average is 3 hours and 23 minutes; this rises significantly in the 16-24-year-old age group, who spend an average of four hours a day looking at their mobiles.

♦ Half of the UK's smartphone users are planning to reduce their screen time this year.

♦ 44.25 per cent of the 2,077 people surveyed said they were 'definitely happy' with the amount of time they spend looking at their phone each day.

The national poll was carried out by digital agency Code Computerlove

Time well spent?

To delve deeper into how people are racking up so much time on their phones, the poll explored screen time activities. The top five included messaging friends & family (67%), browsing social media (59%), reading the news (48%), watching & listening to music (49%) and online shopping (35%).

Interestingly, people are twice as likely to browse (59%) than post (30%) on social media, indicating these platforms are often used in quite a passive way.

12% of people say they take selfies at least once a day on their phones – the figure is slightly higher for males (12.15%) than females (11.67%). Perhaps unsurprisingly 16-24s are the most active selfie-takers, at 25 per cent. This is compared to two per cent of over-55s.

Daily usage of health/fitness apps is somewhat common (17%), but other 'healthy' types of apps are only used by a small minority: Sleep improvement (6%), Meditation (6%), Producing music / creating art (5%) and Journaling (4%).

Anywhere, any time – even on the loo!

The convenience of smartphones means we can chat, shop and scroll almost anywhere – in fact, one in three people use their phones whilst on the toilet.

But it seems one device isn't enough for screen-happy Brits; the most common situation in which people use their smartphones is while watching TV (64% use their mobiles in front of the telly). This was followed closely by people using their devices in bed (55%), both morning and night. Other top answers were on the bus or train (34%) and at work (33%).

More accountability needed for UK's digital wellbeing, say Brits

As well as smartphone users planning to take more personal responsibility for managing their screen time, the survey also revealed that 58 per cent of people feel that companies and social media businesses should be accountable for delivering 'responsible tech' and helping people to reduce their screen time.

How do people spend time online?

messaging friends & family
67%

browsing social media
59%

reading the news
48%

watching & listening to music
49%

online shopping
35%

Source: Code Computerlove

Where do people spend time online?

while watching TV
64%

in bed
55%

on the bus or train
34%

at work
33%

But it's not all bad news for digital technology and smartphone manufacturers.

Interestingly, despite large numbers of people reporting that they want to reduce their screen time in 2019, when asked to reflect on the feelings evoked by their smartphone usage, positive responses dominated.

A feeling of 'connection' came out as the top response (38%) followed closely by satisfaction (37%). Empowerment (16%) and gratitude (15%) were other positive emotions relating to smartphone usage.

The numbers reporting negative feelings were lower – guilt (13%), anxiety (11%), shame (9%) and despair (5%).

Code Computerlove carried out the survey to gather more insight into attitudes around digital wellbeing. Code's Managing Director, Louis Georgiou, said:

'There is so much debate around the impacts of smartphone usage, but not as much around screen time specifically. The survey has given us much greater insight into how much time is actually spent on these devices, how people feel about their own habits – both the negatives and the positives – and, in turn, the need for businesses to create digital experiences that support, rather than undermine, people's wellbeing.

'While some of the findings are quite shocking, such as how long some demographics spend on their phones, the positive attitudes towards owning a device outweigh the negatives – good news for many. It is worth noting, though, that the majority of those asked said that companies have a duty to deliver 'responsible tech', and that people are tracking their screen time to try and reduce it in the future.'

Also commenting on the findings, Dr Taljinder Basra, HCPC Registered Clinical and Forensic Psychologist, said: 'There is very little robust UK research available that explores the psychological factors associated with excessive smartphone use.

'There is likely to be a number of hypotheses, such as smartphones may provide a sense of belonging, a sense of connectedness, a way to get access to information quickly and effortlessly and they are a much easier means to communicate. But why people may go from 'normal' use to excessive 'compulsive/addictive' use and the psychological implications of this is relatively unknown and in the early infancy of research.

'By their very nature, smartphones are multi-faceted – their functionality makes them attractive to use and before you know it, you've been on the device for hours! It is not yet clear whether people become excessive users due to this multifaceted functionality or whether excessive use is related to certain media types.'

Dr Adam Galpin, Psychology lecturer at the School of Health & Society, University of Salford, added: 'This large, nationally representative sample reveals some really interesting demographic patterns related to how people perceive their phone use. What comes through very strongly is how experiences shift with age: young people use their phone more, are more likely to report feeling stressed as a consequence, and are more likely to seek out ways to reduce negative impact through a digital detox or tracking their own screen time.

'These findings add to the evidence on screen time and digital well-being by revealing how people perceive the effects of the phone use on their own well-being and how this shifts across the lifespan.'

4 April 2019

Moderate levels of screen time can be good for children's wellbeing, new research finds

The study was based on data collected from more than 35,000 US children.

By Rhiannon Williams

Spending a moderate amount of time using electronic devices each day could have a positive effect on children's wellbeing and mental health, a new study has found.

Children who spend between one and two hours a day watching television or playing on devices including smartphones, tablets, computers and video games consoles are more likely to demonstrate higher levels of 'psychosocial' functioning than children exposed to no screen time, researchers from the Oxford Internet Institute at Oxford University claimed.

The research, carried out in partnership with Cardiff University and Cambridge University and published in the Journal of the American Academy of Child & Adolescent Psychiatry, suggested that children who experience a moderate amount of screen time exposure are likely to possess better levels of emotional and social wellbeing than non-users.

Professor Andrew Przybylski, director of research at the Oxford Internet Institute, said the study, based on data from more than 35,000 children and their caregivers in America, was undertaken to address the 'precautionary' measures given to parents and teachers as professional advice over appropriate levels of screentime.

The advice, which has been 'predominately shaped by a sense of precaution that prioritises limits on digital engagement', is a result of a lack of compelling evidence linking digital screen engagement to mental and physical wellbeing, he said.

'Very few children, if any, routinely use television and device-based screens enough, on average, to show significantly lower levels of psychological functioning,' he explained.

'Instead, these findings indicate that other aspects of digital engagement, including what is on screens and how caregivers moderate their use, are far more important.'

Screen time concerns

The children's parents or carers completed questionnaires about their child's screen time use, providing details of how much time they spent using the devices each day. They also relayed how much time the children had spent using the devices before 'psychosocial functioning problems' were detected.

The children spent over four hours watching TV and more than five hours interacting with devices before they displayed what the study characterised as 'functioning difficulties'.

They spent an average of one hour 41 minutes engaged in TV-based activities, categorised as gaming or watching films, and one hour 53 minutes on average using tablets and smartphones.

Separate research from the University of Alberta linked two or more hours of screen time each day to 'clinically significant behavioural problems', including inattention, compared to those watching under 30 minutes daily.

The study, which was published in April, examined close to 3,500 children in Canada, and found that children exposed to more screen time at either three or five years old demonstrated 'significantly greater behavioural and attention problems at age five'.

The World Health Organisation (WHO) recommends babies and toddlers under the age of two years should not be left to passively watch TV or other screens.

Children aged between two and five years old should not exceed one hour of screen time daily, the body said in April, adding: 'less is better'.

24 October 2019

Internet is giving us shorter attention spans and worse memories, major study suggests

The major study by top universities across the world looked at how the internet is shaping our brains.

By Mike Wright, social media correspondent and Ellie Zolfagharifard

Using the internet is physically changing our brains so that we have shorter attention spans and worse memory, major study has suggested.

A review by academics from Oxford, King's College London, Harvard and Western Sydney University, found smartphones were also replacing our ability to remember facts while tricking us into thinking we are smarter than we actually are.

The findings come after a global team reviewed scores of studies and experiments to assess the impact the internet has had on our brains over the last three decades.

It comes as earlier this month Ofcom found that the average British adult is now spending 50 whole days a year online.

Dr Joseph Firth, Senior Research Fellow at Western Sydney University, said: 'The key findings of this report are that high-levels of Internet use could indeed impact on many functions of the brain.

'For example, the limitless stream of prompts and notifications from the internet encourages us towards constantly holding a divided attention – which then in turn may decrease our capacity for maintaining concentration on a single task.'

Experiments reviewed in the study showed that people who spent their time constantly flipping between short activities online 'require greater cognitive effort to maintain concentration'.

The endless stream of notifications and digital distractions were found to be physically influencing the brain, with those affected showing less grey matter in the cerebral areas associated with maintaining focus.

Other studies showed the internet having an immediate impact on our ability to concentrate, with people displaying a reduced capacity to maintain attention after activities such as internet shopping. Whereas offline activities such as reading a magazine showed no such impact.

Multitasking online was even found to make people less effective at multitasking offline. The study said: 'Overall, the available evidence strongly indicates that engaging in multi-tasking via digital media does not improve our multi-tasking performance in other settings – and in fact seems to decrease this cognitive capacity through reducing our ability to ignore incoming distractions.'

As well as making us more distracted, the study found evidence that the internet was becoming our 'external memory' as we relied more and more on smartphones to retrieve information. However, instead of learning new facts gleaned online the brain tended to instead log where to find the information on the internet.

One experiment cited showed that a group of people searching online found information faster than another using encyclopedias, but were less able to recall the information accurately.

Other studies showed that the internet was also deceiving people into thinking they were smarter than they are as they 'blurred the lines' between their own memories and what they can easily look up on ever-present smartphones.

The report said: 'Results showed that online searching increases our sense of how much we know, even though the illusion of self-knowledge is only perceived for the domains in which the internet can "fill in the gaps" for us.'

The study noted that there could be an upside to this reliance on the internet as a virtual memory in the future, as it could free up brain power for other activities – although it did not speculate what these could be.

Lastly, the academics found that the social side of our brains acted in a very similar way online as offline. Yet, we are being put under new stresses, such as the stark rejection people feel from having social value quantified by the number of friends and likes they receive, as well as constantly comparing ourselves with 'hyper-successful individuals' who are ubiquitous on social media.

6 June 2019

Is the internet good or bad?

In this day and age, it's hard to imagine life without the internet. Accessible via our PCs, laptops, tablets and phones, it has permeated society and transformed the way we go about our day to day business. But is it actually a good thing? DisCUss takes a look at the good and bad points of the worldwide web.

Good: You have an enormous library of information and resources at your fingertips

Bad: Not every source is reliable or trustworthy

How wonderful that almost all of the questions we ponder, from the sensible 'where is my nearest takeaway' to the inane 'what would a chair look like if your knees bent the other way' (actual search), can all be Googled in seconds. The internet is a powerful source of knowledge for all of us, certainly few students could imagine getting though their studies without this amazing research tool.

However, it is important to remember that not everything you see or read on the internet is 100% reliable or genuine. Online encyclopedia giant Wikipedia is a prime example of this: it is created and edited by volunteers around the world, but 'anyone with internet access can write and make changes to Wikipedia articles, except in limited cases where editing is restricted to prevent disruption or vandalism'. Best to keep this in mind before you reference an article in your assignments.

Good: It's really easy to keep abreast of current news and events

Bad: Internet can also be used as a platform to spread negative messages

The internet is a fantastic global resource for current affairs and entertainment news, with many channels now updated in real time. Important campaigns and messages can be promoted, such as health awareness campaigns, so that it reaches a greater audience and ensures we are well-informed. Most news articles now allow readers the option to comment and voice their opinions too, which make us more engaged with the world and sparks interesting debates and viewpoints.

The downside, as with any platform, is that people can also use it to share propaganda and/or inappropriate content. The challenge is trying to control how these messages are spread, as they can reach vulnerable and impressionable audiences.

Good: You can do all your banking online, and shopping on the web is so easy

Bad: Accounts can be hacked into

From food shopping to keeping track of your outgoings, the internet allows us to manage our finances and buy the things we want with relative ease, all without having to venture out of the door. While businesses are constantly developing ways to make your online customer accounts more secure, it is worth remembering that accounts are at risk of being hacked, so ensure your passwords are changed regularly, and where possible, try not to save your card details on shopping accounts.

Good: Social media means I can keep in touch with friends old and new

Bad: Social media changes the way we interact, and not everyone is who they say they are

Social media can sometimes get a bad rap, but we cannot deny it has become a prevalent part of society, and a key tool many of us use to keep in touch with loved ones or expand our virtual social circles. Long distance friendships can be maintained, conversations can be struck up over shared content and we are allowed a glimpse into the lives of others, which will always be a source of fascination.

However many people argue that this is making us lazy in our interactions, and accuse social media users of 'cherry picking' the content they share with friends, so that it makes their lives appear a lot more exciting and glamorous than it really is, inadvertently making others feel inferior (#FOMO).

Good: When you're bored, the internet provides entertainment

Bad: It can become addictive

The internet hosts a plethora of technology and entertainment. Our impatient natures are satisfied by the ability to instantly conjure games, music and videos. It can provide a talking point among friends, keep the kids quiet for hours or provide you with a window of escapism from a stressful day. But have you ever just been scrolling through your Instagram feed or playing a game and then before you know it, it's 2am and you haven't even had your dinner yet? Yeah…we've all been there. Emerging research has indicated that the effects of using technology can mimic those of drugs and alcohol, where the brain's frontal cortex — which controls executive functioning, including impulse control — is affected in exactly the same way as it would be through cocaine use. Technology is so hyper-arousing that it raises dopamine levels — the feel-good neurotransmitter most involved in the addiction dynamic.

Our verdict?

The internet continues to be an enigma: we are still learning about its capabilities, and new ideas are constantly being developed to improve and expand usability. While it's true that some of the negatives can never be completely eliminated, it is fair to say that through education and experience we as a community are gradually becoming savvier. Awareness campaigns surrounding cybersecurity and online conduct are certainly helping us to recognise how to protect ourselves and others online, and recent research has shown a decrease in the amount of time we are spending on sites such as Facebook, perhaps suggesting that the novelties of social media are less overpowering.

What are your thoughts? Do you think the internet has a positive effect on your life?

Parents more concerned about their children online

More parents than ever feel children's online use now carries more risks than benefits, according to Ofcom's latest research into children's media and online lives.

Our *Children's Media Use and Attitudes report 2019* is based on around 3,500 interviews with children and parents. *Children's Media Lives* is a qualitative report looking at how children aged eight to 18 think about and use digital media.

Parents and carers are becoming more likely to trust their children with greater digital independence at a younger age. But far fewer believe the benefits of their child being online outweigh the risks than five years ago. And around two million parents now feel the internet does their children more harm than good.

This comes as children are now more likely to see hateful content online. Half of 12-15s who go online had seen hateful content in the last year, up from a third in 2016.

Parents are increasingly concerned about their child seeing something online which might encourage them to harm themselves. Similarly, two gaming-related problems are increasingly concerning parents: the pressure on their child to make in-game purchases of things like 'loot boxes', a virtual item containing rewards; and the possibility of their child being bullied via online games.

However, parents are now more likely than in 2018 to speak to their children about staying safe online, and are nearly twice as likely to go online themselves for support and information about keeping their children safe.

Influencers, online activism and girl gamers

Looking at what today's children are doing online, we uncovered three big trends over the past year.

♦ 18% of 12 to 15-year-olds use social media to support causes and organisations by sharing or commenting on posts, up from 12% in 2018.

♦ The 'Greta effect'. There is increased online social activism among children. Almost a fifth of 12-15s use social media to express support for causes and organisations by sharing or commenting on posts. One in 10 signed petitions on social media.

♦ Rise of the 'vlogger next door'. While high-profile YouTube stars remain popular, children are now increasingly drawn to so-called 'micro' or 'nano' influencers. These often have fewer followers, but might be local to a child's area or share a niche interest.

♦ Girl gamers on the increase. Almost half of girls aged five to 15 now play games online – up from 39% in 2018. The proportion of boy gamers is unchanged at 71%, but boys spend twice as long playing online each week as girls.

Social media use more fragmented

The proportion of 12 to 15-year-olds who have a social media profile on Facebook (69%), Snapchat (68%), Instagram (66%), WhatsApp (62%), YouTube (47%), Pinterest (13%), TikTok (13%) and Twitch (5%). Older children are using a wider range of social media platforms than ever before. WhatsApp

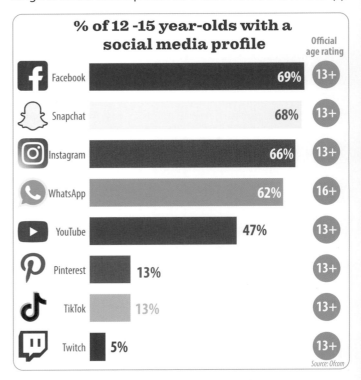

% of 12-15 year-olds with a social media profile

Platform	%	Official age rating
Facebook	69%	13+
Snapchat	68%	13+
Instagram	66%	13+
WhatsApp	62%	16+
YouTube	47%	13+
Pinterest	13%	13+
TikTok	13%	13+
Twitch	5%	13+

Source: Ofcom

in particular has grown in popularity among 12 to 15-year-olds since last year, despite having a minimum age limit of 16.

WhatsApp is now used by almost two thirds of older children – up from 43% in 2018. For the first time, it rivals Facebook, Snapchat and Instagram as one of the top social media platforms for older children.

Newer platforms are also becoming more popular. Around one in seven older children use TikTok, which enables users to create and upload lip-sync, comedy and talent videos, while one in 20 older children uses Twitch, a live streaming platform for gamers.

18% of 12-15 year-olds use social media to support causes and organisations by sharing or commenting on posts

Increased from 12% in 2019

Source: Ofcom

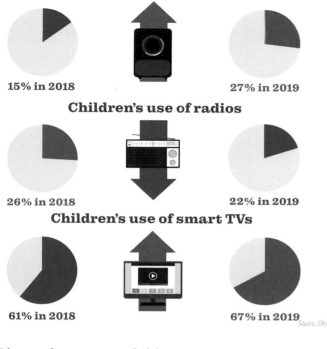

Children's use of smart speakers

15% in 2018   27% in 2019

Children's use of radios

26% in 2018   22% in 2019

Children's use of smart TVs

61% in 2018   67% in 2019

Source: Ofcom

Alexa – how many children use smart speakers?

Children are using more connected devices than ever before. Among these, smart speakers saw the biggest increase over the past year, with more than a quarter of children now using them. Children's use of smart TVs also increased.

Children's viewing habits are changing radically too. Almost twice as many children watch streaming content than they did five years ago. In 2019, fewer children watched traditional broadcast TV than streaming content, with a quarter not watching it at all.

But YouTube is as popular as ever, remaining children's firm favourite for video ahead of Netflix, Amazon Prime, the BBC and ITV.

The age of digital independence

50% of 10 year-olds own a smartphone in 2019, up from 30% in 2015. When it comes to going online, children are most likely to use a tablet but mobiles are becoming increasingly popular and children are now as likely to use a mobile as they are a laptop.

This move to mobile is being driven by older children, for whom 10 is becoming the age of digital independence. Between age nine and 10, the proportion of children who own a smartphone doubles to 50% – giving them greater digital freedom as they prepare to move to secondary school. By the time they are 15, almost all children have one.

The proportion of children who own their own smartphones or tablets increases with age. Up until they turn ten, children are more likely to own tablets. However, between the ages of nine and ten, smartphone ownership doubles from 23% to 50%

'Today's children have never known life without the internet, but two million parents now feel the internet causes them more harm than good.

'So it's encouraging that parents, carers and teachers are now having more conversations than ever before with children about online safety. Education and stronger regulation will also help children to embrace their digital independence, while protecting them from the risks.'

Yih-Choung Teh, Ofcom's Strategy and Research Group Director

4 February 2020

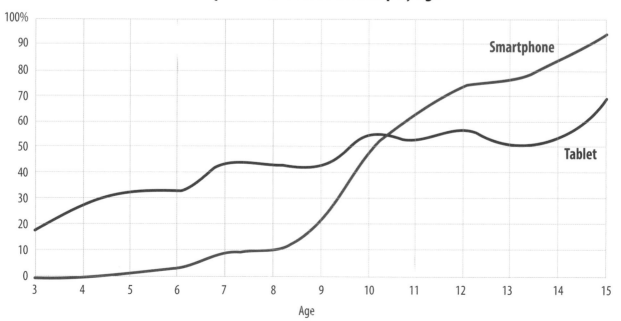

Smartphone vs, tablet ownership by age

Smartphone

Tablet

Age

Source: Ofcom

Children's experiences of online harm and what they want to do about it

By Elizabeth Reeves, Policy and Advocacy

In April this year the Government set out their plans for a world-first: a system of regulations that they argue will make the UK 'the safest place in the world to be online'. The Online Harms White Paper, produced in collaboration between the Home Office and Department for Digital, Culture, Media and Sport (DCMS), maps out the UK's plan to hold web giants to account for a broad range of online harms. The 'harms' targeted by the white paper are vast in scope, numbering 23 in total and covering topics as serious and diverse as modern slavery, terrorism, child sexting and abuse. The aim of these measures is to create a safe online space for all users, including children and young people, where they can feel free to communicate, research and play.

The Children's Commissioner's challenge to the Government was to ensure these measures are truly informed by voices and opinions of children. Today's kids were born into an online world that they did not create; an inescapable reality of 24-hour connection, entertainment and social pressure. It is the responsibility of adults to ensure that children have the greatest possible power to shape this first iteration of digital regulation.

In January, Jeremy Wright (then Secretary of State for Digital, Culture, Media and Sport) asked the Children's Commissioner's Office to join forces with the Department to help them consult with children themselves. We worked with DCMS to set up and facilitate two workshops with groups from primary and secondary schools. We devised the workshops to find out how these children and young people feel about the current state of affairs online, and the Government's proposals to change the rulebook

We asked the children who participated whether they had, themselves, been exposed to disturbing, abusive or potentially illegal content while online. The reaction in both groups was an overwhelming 'yes' – particularly on social media and while gaming with anonymous, often older players.

'It makes you feel like they don't care if they don't respond'

Many of the children had reported instances of harmful content, whether to social media or gaming platforms. However, many told us that the system was confusing, impersonal and rarely had any effect:

'Any reports I have made are generally not responded to…I may have been responded to once, but I can't really remember a clear time I was answered' – Secondary school child

'It makes you feel like they don't care if they don't respond' – Primary school child

'Every person's report should be taken seriously and once something has been done about it, the user should be informed' – Secondary school child

The younger students told us that the reporting process could be difficult for them to navigate:

'I think they should make it more simple so that you can call up for reports instead of having to type' – Primary school child

'You don't know if they are robots when you contact them' – Primary school child

Reporting makes things worse

The children were particularly keen to discuss the often violent nature of many online gaming platforms, and the potential repercussions of reporting abusive behaviour:

'Once someone kept on swearing because I died' – Primary school child

'Reporting makes things worse in the gaming area' – Secondary school child

Several children told us that, due to a lack of anonymity on several mainstream games, reporting bad behaviour only multiplied abuse from other players. They told us that reporting during a game was seen as being 'weak' or a 'sore loser', allowing aggressive and abusive environments to thrive.

How do young people respond to a lack of a safe, effective, anonymous reporting system on social media and within their games? The children we asked told us that they resorted to blocking or confronting users themselves or sought help from trusted adults. In the most extreme cases they deleted the game or app.

'I would stop playing and play a less mainstream game' – Senior school child

'I would delete the game but not download it again. I would tell my parents and look for a different game' – Primary school child

Companies that breach their duty of care

We presented the children with a selection of four proposals, set out in the White Paper, for how to deal with companies that breach their duty of care to users of their platforms. The groups split into pairs and ranked the following policies, from one (favourite) to four (least favourite):

♦ Pay a fine

♦ Have to say what they are doing to fix the problem

♦ The site should be blocked so that no one can use it anymore

♦ The senior managers of the company should be held responsible

Most senior school children wanted sites to say what they were doing to fix the problem, revealing their desire for more transparency from companies and a greater sense of influence over their decisions.

The Primary school children, on the whole, favoured the most extreme option: blocking the site altogether. This demonstrated to us the strength of feeling among the youngest users of the internet, and their desire for something to be done to change the status quo.

Notably the children generally liked all four policies, and felt that all options should be open to the regulator and be used in conjunction with one another.

'[School] just keep telling us the same thing'

When asked how they learn to stay safe online, both groups were relatively critical of their safety lessons, feeling disengaged by lengthy and repetitive talks:

'I don't think that e-safety day tells us anything at school because they just keep telling us the same thing' – Primary school child

'They don't show us how to where to block. We always do a poster but it doesn't really help us!' – Primary school child

They want creative and engaging online safety sessions, as well as teaching from individuals with relevant personal experience:

'The government should fund smaller projects and cleverer ways to show the information' – Secondary school child

'Workshops! Class-size workshops or larger – asking questions and discussing responses to different scenarios. Good atmosphere, not too serious but informative' – Secondary school child

The young people also wanted more education around technical and legal issues, such as reporting, data collection, privacy and how to interpret T&Cs:

'I click everything and don't read terms and conditions as they are too long, they should make simple rules for children not so long' – Primary school child

'Knowing how to respond to toxic comments when reporting doesn't work or isn't responded to (which is often)' – Secondary school child

'Learning about how companies collect data for customised advertising; privacy and what companies use your info for' – Secondary school child)

The most interesting and crucial findings from these focus groups were around gaming. It seems that gaming is just as, if not more important to children than social media – and that seemed true for the older kids as well as the younger ones. Furthermore, children's experiences of gaming sometimes differ from social media. For example, children seemed a lot more reluctant to report on the former compared to the latter.

It's clear from the children we spoke with that online harms legislation works across different types of platform – especially gaming sites – and we will continue to talk to DCMS and the Home Office as legislation evolves.

The Children's Commissioner's Office is also working on a new project looking at the benefits and drawbacks of online gaming, to better understand children's experiences in this rapidly developing field, to be published later this year.

27 August 2019

Online abuse: teenagers might not report it because they often don't see it as a problem

An article from *The Conversation*.

THE CONVERSATION

By Holly Powell-Jones, Lecturer in Criminology and Media Law, City, University of London

Protecting children from harm online is high on the political agenda right now. The UK government has set out plans to make social media companies legally responsible for protecting users, and MPs have criticised social media platforms for relying on users to report abuse.

This is a serious problem, especially if people who come across illegal material online don't recognise it as such. While working as a news presenter, I helped run a project teaching thousands of children about social media laws and I noticed patterns emerging in their responses to threatening, abusive and hateful messages online. They said things like:

> *You're not physically doing anything. Things like this are said all the time. You can't arrest everyone on the internet.*
>
> *– Year 12 pupil.*

> *Even though it's disgusting, as long as there's no physical violence, it's okay. Free speech. It's an opinion.*
>
> *– Year 13 pupil.*

> *Don't think you could be arrested … Nothing happens on social media, no one gets into trouble, so many people say bad stuff. –*
>
> *Year 8 pupil.*

So, in 2014, I began an academic study giving 184 participants – aged 11 to 18 – different examples of social media posts, and asking them how 'risky' they were, in terms of whether the person posting them might get in trouble.

Among the examples (informed by Crown Prosecution Service guidelines) were racist, homophobic and misogynistic material; threats of violence; potential harassment and a post suggesting image-based sexual abuse (commonly called 'revenge porn').

I asked young people to think of the different levels of risk like traffic lights: red for criminal risk (police involvement), orange for civil risk (legal action by other people), yellow for social risk (sanctions from school or family) and green for no risk. I also asked them why they thought abusive posts might not be a criminal risk. Here's what I found.

Victim blaming

One example I used was a post which seemed to share a sexual video of a fictional person called 'Alice' (signified as comments with a link to a YouTube video). This created more disagreement than any other example, as different participants put it under all four categories of risk. This is surprising, given that schools, the media and non-governmental organisations have all emphasised the risks of sharing indecent images. It's even included in the Department of Education's new guidelines for sex education.

Even so, some children argued a sender 'couldn't be in trouble' if Alice had agreed to the video in the first place – without even questioning whether she might have been pressured into it, which studies reveal is a common occurrence among young people. Indeed, even if Alice had consented to be filmed, sharing the video without her permission could still be illegal under two different laws, depending on whether she was under 18 or not.

Victim blaming is used as a way to downplay the responsibility of the people who share such content online. It also implies that victims should 'just deal with it' themselves. In fact, the children in my study thought it more likely that Alice would sue a sender privately, than involve the police.

Defending free speech

'Just saying', 'just joking' and 'just an opinion' were common responses to online posts in my study – even to hate speech or threats, which could actually result in a criminal conviction. Freedom of speech can be wrongly viewed as a 'catch-all' right for people to say whatever they like online. In some cases, children's views mimicked alt-right arguments in favour of liberty, free speech and the right to offend.

In reality, freedom of expression has always had legal limits, and material inciting hatred and violence on the grounds of race, religion or sexual orientation is criminalised under the Public Order Act 1986.

Some teens believed even jokes had their limits, though – and most thought a joke bomb threat would result in prison. It's ironic that this was the post that most of my participants agreed would lead to prison, given that someone was famously acquitted for a similar tweet in 2012.

Tolerating abuse

Many children doubted there would be any serious consequences for social media abusers – a finding echoed in other studies. Some felt police wouldn't 'waste time' dealing with cyber-hate – which news reports suggest is probably accurate.

Others argued that hateful or threatening content is 'tolerated' on social media, and so widespread as to be 'normal'. And given the scale of online abuse against women, for example, they may have a point.

Younger children were more likely to think that police might get involved, whereas older teens put abusive posts in lower risk categories. It's possible that as children grow up and spend more time online, they see a larger amount of abusive material shared without any obvious consequences, and assume it can't be illegal. This is bad news for young people who might repost or share abuse, but also for victims, who may think there's no point seeking support.

Anything goes?

It's often claimed we live in a 'post-truth ' or 'post-moral' society. There wasn't much debate over who was correct within my focus groups. Despite the lack of agreement between the children, different viewpoints were seen as 'equally valid'. Respecting others' arguments is one thing, but failing to tell truth from lies is also a cause for concern.

Young people need to be given the tools they need to understand and critique arguments based on reliable evidence. Universal human rights are a good starting point for lawmakers to try to reach global agreement on what will (or won't) be tolerated online. But young people also need to be educated to understand those rights. Otherwise, social media sites could simply become a space where there are no recognised victims or offenders, a place where – morally speaking – anything goes.

7 May 2019

The government should actually understand the internet if it's going to protect kids from online harms

This approach to safer internet use for children is as misguided as 1960s fears about TV. We have to shape policy around the lives and perspectives of young people.

By Amy Orben

A world with less child abuse content, terrorist materials and self-harm images is a world worth striving for. This week's publication of the government's strategy against so-called 'online harms' (i.e. to give Ofcom responsibility over policing online content) is therefore a long-overdue step. If only it were more informed.

The policy proposal makes it painfully clear how little we currently know about the effects of new technologies; technologies that we, and our children, use for many happy and productive hours every day.

Our current system for understanding and regulating such innovations, the same one employed to deliver the online harms strategy, is not fit for purpose – it is outpaced by a fast-moving, highly individualised technological space. And these are the obstacles that are holding back our ability to react assertively to such accelerating technological change.

Firstly, the current focus on screen time is misguided. Sonia Livingstone, LSE professor, supports this in a report published this week to mark Safer Internet Day; she points out that parents' fears about three areas – content, contact and conduct – have little to do with the duration of 'screen time'. The internet now provides children with a greater variety of uses, content and activities than ever, and time is not an appropriate measure for any of those.

The focus of the government's new policies on 'online harms' might, therefore, be a welcome change for parents, the NSPCC and other organisations campaigning for a safer internet.

Yet while it is relatively clear how self-harm images, radicalised content and child pornography are harmful, there could be many other aspects of the online world that are causing individual or general harm: for example, design

features, algorithmic biases, and the tracking of behaviour across platforms.

In her report, Livingstone quotes Wilbur Schramm's 1961 reflections on the early days of television: 'For some children, under some conditions, some television is harmful. For some children under the same conditions, or for the same children under other conditions, it may be beneficial. For most children, under most conditions, most television is probably neither particularly harmful nor particularly beneficial.' If we replace 'television' with 'internet' in this quote, we have an accurate representation of research today.

It is currently impossible to identify anything except the most obvious of online harms. And what might be harmful to some, could be beneficial to others.

Had there been a concentrated conversation about this when development began on the Online Harms White Paper two years ago, many pertinent questions would have emerged.

The first of these questions is about access to data. While huge amounts of rich data about our online activities are tracked in real time, these data are owned by companies which have little incentive to make them available for research. Even academic researchers – in the UK or anywhere else – are routinely excluded despite needing the data as raw materials to provide important evidence.

As I have found in my work, the lack of data access means researchers often need to rely on children's (or parents') own estimates of their time spent online to understand technology effects. This makes it impossible to provide detailed insights about anything other than 'screen time' or other vague notions of time spent on different platforms.

The government wants children growing up in the UK to have the world's best safeguards against online harms. However, policy makers and regulators need to be furnished with high-quality, objective research.

Academic research is heavily curtailed, and politicians are delaying important decisions as a result. If the regulator doesn't want to be playing catch up with the tech giants for the next few decades, this will have to change. A much closer relationship between academics and policy, and more initiatives to ensure controlled and ethical data-sharing, transparent practices and real-time collaboration between scientists and the tech industry are needed.

The British Academy, the national body for the humanities and social sciences, says debates over childhood policy currently give us an important opportunity for policy to draw on valuable research and protect the most vulnerable from harm.

The first step is to shape policy around the lives and perspectives of children. Where parents see 'screen time', academics might see a far richer variety of different activities children are engaging in, some harmful and some beneficial, e.g. doing homework, skyping relatives, watching TV programmes, reading horror stories or starting mindfulness meditation.

With more well-rounded research and closer links to policy, we may discover more about the extent to which online risks can lead to harm, as well as understanding the opportunities new technologies provide.

As it stands, research is highlighting that social media and digital technology are not as harmful as often feared. But when a more harmful technology arrives, the current system for understanding and reacting to it would be outmanoeuvred. This is where the real risks lie.

15 February 2020

EU Kids Online 2020 finds more risk to children online, but not always more harm

By Sonia Livingstone

For Safer Internet Day 2020, a new report, EU Kids Online 2020: Survey results from 19 countries, has mapped the risks and opportunities of the internet for children in Europe. For the report, researchers from the EU Kids Online network collaborated between autumn 2017 and summer 2019 to conduct a major survey of 25,101 children aged 9-16 in 19 European countries.

Screen time problems?

Most European children use a smartphones 'daily' or 'almost all the time,' and devices are changing too, as the report documents. For example, in most countries less than half of children aged 9-16 access the internet through a desktop computer or notebook, 3-13% (depending on the country) connect though a wearable device, and 1-18% via a connected toy.

The survey shows that compared with the EU Kids Online 2010 survey, the time children spend online each day has almost doubled in many countries – for example, from about one to three hours per day in Spain, and from about two to three-and-a-half hours in Norway. This may explain why parental anxieties about screen time are high.

However, we have argued elsewhere on this blog that it is timely to shift the focus from a count of hours to a more contextual assessment of the quality and nature of children's engagement with digital media. In support of this proposal, and contra anxieties about 'internet addiction,' the survey showed that few children say they have gone without eating and sleeping because of their internet use, though more – ranging from 4% (Slovakia) to 19% (Malta) – said that they have spent less time with family, friends or doing schoolwork because of time spent online. Overall, the majority of children in all countries said that none of these possible consequences of excessive internet use applied to them, and less than 2% reported all five consequences.

Risks and harms

Beyond questions about screen time, parents are anxious about content, contact and conduct risks that their children may encounter online. The EU Kids Online 2020 report has lots of statistics on these risks, showing considerable variation by country. However, the EU Kids Online network has long argued that while online risk carries a probability of harm to a child, this is not inevitable. Many factors can make a child more resilient or vulnerable to the consequences of exposure to risk.

In the survey, children were asked to give an overall view of online harms, in answer to the question:

'In the past year, has anything ever happened online that bothered or upset you in some way (e.g., made you feel upset, uncomfortable, scared or that you shouldn't have seen it)?'

The number of online risks (out of 7) encountered by 12 to 16 year olds, and the proportion who report being upset or bothered online in the past year, by country

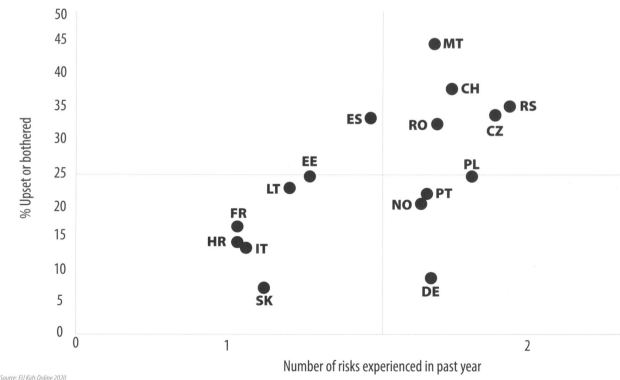

Source: EU Kids Online 2020

The percentage of children who reported that they had been bothered or upset on the internet in 2020 varied by country from 7% (Slovakia) to 45% (Malta), a notable increase from 2010 when the range was from 6% to 25% across countries. Interestingly, the proportion of children who said something online had bothered or upset them is smaller than the proportions in each country who reported more common risks. This suggests that not all risk results in self-reported harm to a child.

Complicating matters further, the findings suggest that the same activity can have positive consequences for one child and negative for another. One example is meeting new people online. Between 5% (France) and 25% (Serbia) of the children met someone face-to-face that they had only known online. For the majority, meeting new people was positive and exciting: between 52% (Slovakia) and 86% (Romania) of the children who met with someone they knew online said that they were happy after such a meeting. But for others, such an experience could cause distress and potential harm: in most of the countries, less than 5% of those who went to such a meeting said that they were fairly or very upset.

Going deeper into the findings, the survey also found national variation in the relation between risk and harm. In the graph (Figure 1), the horizontal dimension shows variation in how many risks children in a country reported in the past year, on average, measured out of the seven risks we asked about. As may be seen, children in Croatia reported the fewest risks, and children in Russia the most. The vertical dimension shows the percentage of children who reported being upset by something online in the past year, with fewest children in Slovakia and most children in Malta saying 'yes' this happened to them.

Clearly there is a broadly positive association between the two measures – the more risks, the more harm, as children report it. Yet there is also a lot of variation that invites further investigation. For example, children in Germany report more risks than those in Slovakia yet no more harm: possibly, the safer internet provision in Germany is greater, so that encountering risk is less likely to result in children being upset, by comparison with the situation in Slovakia. Overall, we see one group of countries where higher risk is not linked to more harm – Germany, Norway, Portugal. Then there are countries where even just a few risks are linked to more harm – Estonia and Spain in particular.

While certainly the countries where both risk and harm are highest (the top right quadrant) merit investigation and possible intervention, our point is that policy interventions should focus more on reducing harm than risk. This is because children cannot develop resilience if they are protected from all forms of risk and, further, such protections are often achieved by limiting children's online opportunities. In other words, there may be much to be learned from countries in which children encounter as much risk, but less harm, than in other countries. Do those countries practise more parental mediation? Or have they better regulation of platforms? Or a culture of respecting children's expression of concern and of providing help?

From research to understanding and action

Even basic descriptive statistics can serve to counter myths, challenge media panics and, more positively, ground interventions in policy and practice by providing estimates of prevalence. For example, the degree to which children are exposed to risk online is shown to be rather less than sometimes feared by parents or claimed by the mass media. This does not warrant the claim that nothing should be done, but it invites a careful assessment of priorities, and a weighing of the consequences of different kinds of interventions.

A holistic approach to children's wellbeing is often called for but less easy to deliver. It is still the case that most researchers and policy makers concentrate either on the opportunities of a digital world – concerned with education or civic participation or creative expression, for example – or on the risks of harm to children – concerned with e-safety, parental mediation or internet regulation. Achieving a holistic approach – whether at the level of a country or culture, or for an individual child – remains challenging. Those excited by digital opportunities still tend to neglect or postpone the ways in which increasing opportunities tends to go hand-in-hand with increasing the risks of the digital world for children. Those who prioritise child protection and safety can struggle to realise that their interventions may also serve to limit children's civil rights and freedoms.

Hopefully, the findings in this report provide both some pointers as to where to focus action, and a benchmark against which to measure progress.

11 February 2020

The ten internet dangers to kids – and how you can stop them

The danger is the ease and speed with which children could be exposed to inappropriate content that can and will cause psychological and emotional harm.

In today's increasingly digital society, we are only ever a reach away from a device or tablet that can connect us to the world. Whilst this constant link offers lots of opportunities, it also presents a number of dangers – especially to youngsters, who are often left alone with their parents' devices.

Results from a new survey by Kaspersky Lab show that a huge 87 per cent of parents admit that they don't restrict how much time their young children spend online. Three-year-olds are spending more than four hours a week with these 'digital babysitters' and are only ever three seconds from danger, given the size of the average home and the amount of devices within it.

The danger is the ease and speed with which children could be exposed to inappropriate content that can and will cause psychological and emotional harm.

When it comes to the physical security of a child, parents take this very seriously: Kaspersky Lab's investigation revealed that 75 per cent of parents put up a stairgate before their child turns three and 57 per cent put locks on their kitchen cupboards. Worryingly, however, only a very small proportion – just 13 per cent – restrict how much time that children of this age group spend online. This rises just slightly to 33 per cent for four to seven year olds.

These figures show that there is a significant discrepancy in the ways that parents of young children protect them from harm through both physical and digital environments.

Here David Emm, Principal Security Researcher at Kaspersky Lab, outlines the top ten dangers to children – and what parents can do to protect against these dangers.

Inappropriate content

The average child spends 40 minutes per day, or 4.6 hours a week, watching online video content on a mobile device. Yet only 13 per cent of parents install online security on their smartphone, laptop or tablet – and 49 per cent have never reviewed the default settings to prevent their child from viewing inappropriate material. Examining YouTube's suggested videos, which sit visibly alongside clips or episodes of popular children's television programmes such as Peppa Pig, children are just clicks away from content aimed at a more mature audience – featuring violence, guns and nudity.

Use the parental control features in your online security product to block access to sites you don't want your child looking at – it's an easy way to avoid disaster.

Default device settings

As the devices we use on a day-to-day basis become smarter, they also become a bigger threat – offering surveillance opportunities for cybercriminals looking to infiltrate our lives and exploit the information that they find.

Review the default settings on each app that your child uses to ensure that the camera or microphone, for example, aren't automatically turned on as these can pose a threat.

The number of devices in the home

With smart devices encompassing almost every area of our daily existence, we have never been more surrounded by technology. But alarmingly, this demand for connected devices means that children are only ever three seconds away from potential online danger. Take the average size of the UK house, divide it by the number of digital devices, and a child has access to an internet enabled device every 6.9m – taking only 3 seconds for the average toddler to reach one.

Supervise your child's internet use. Encourage them to visit and stay on websites you're familiar with. If you have any concerns, look at their browsing history. Be sure to know about any password-protected sites they may be accessing and ask them to share their login details with you. Encourage your child to be open about what they are doing online and who they are socialising with. Promote a culture of safety within the home and talk openly about the possible dangers which exist.

Cyber-bullying

According to Internetsafety101.org, 90 percent of teens who participate in social media have ignored bullying that they've witnessed online, and one third have been victims of cyber-bullying themselves. Social media and online games are today's virtual playground, and that is where the majority of cyber-bullying takes place. For example, children can be mocked in social media exchanges. Or, in online games, they or their 'player characters' can be subjected to incessant attack, turning the game from an imaginative adventure into a humiliating ordeal.

The best foundation for protecting against cyber-bullying is to be comfortable talking to your children about what is going on in their lives, and how to stand up to bullies.

Cyber-predators

Sexual and other predators can use the internet to target vulnerable children, taking advantage of children's innocence, abusing their trust and, perhaps, ultimately luring them into a very dangerous situation. These predators lurk on social media and game sites that appeal to children (the same virtual playgrounds where cyber-bullying happens). There, they can exploit not only children's innocence, but also their gift of imagination. 'Let's play pretend' is a common and healthy part of online gaming and interaction, but predators can use it as a hook to pull children in.

Thinkuknow offers guidance in safeguarding against predators and other online risks to child safety. However, again, the best protection is to be able to talk to your children about what is happening in their lives.

Posting private information

Children do not yet understand social boundaries. They may post personal information online, for example in their social media profiles, that should not be out in the public domain. This might be anything from images of awkward personal moments to their home addresses.

If your children are posting in public view, you can also see it — and there's no harm in reminding them that if you can see it, so can everyone else. Don't snoop, but talk to your children about public boundaries.

Phishing

Phishing is what cyber-security professionals call the use of email or other messages that try to trick people into clicking on malicious links or attachments. ('Hey — thought you might like this!') This can also be done with malicious text messages (sometimes known as 'smishing').

Phishing emails and smishing texts can pop up at any time, but the cybercriminals who devise them keep watch on sites that are popular with children and can gather information such as email addresses and friends' names to use in their scams.

Teach your children to avoid clicking on emails or texts from strangers and to be wary of messages that claim to be from their friends but have no genuine personal message attached.

Falling for scams

Children are probably not going to fall for Nigerian princes offering them a million dollars, but they might fall for scams that offer things they may prize, such as free access to online games. Young people are easy marks for scams because they have not yet learned to be wary. As with phishing, cybercriminals can use sites popular with children to identify potential victims, and then promise them something in return for what they want — like parents' credit card information.

For young or old, the best protection against scams is knowing that if an offer sounds too good to be true, it probably is. Teach your children to be wary of online offers that promise too much.

Accidentally downloading malware

Malware is computer software that is installed without the knowledge or permission of the victim and performs harmful actions on their computer or other devices. This includes stealing personal information or hijacking the device for use in a 'botnet', which causes sluggish performance. Cybercriminals often trick people into downloading malware. Phishing is one such trick, but there are others — such as convincing victims to download purported games — that can be especially beguiling to children.

As with scams, educating your children is the best protection, but anti-virus software and related security protections can help safeguard your family's devices against malware. In addition, many Internet security products also include specific parental controls that can help you set a secure framework for your children's online activities.

Posts that come back to haunt a child later in life

The Internet does not have a delete key. Anything your child puts online is nearly impossible to remove later. But teenagers in particular are not thinking about how a future boss or partner might respond to 'amusing' images or other personal content that they post to their social media profiles or other websites.

Explain to your teens that if they change how they wish to portray themselves online later, the Internet might not let them.

The Internet can pose dangers to children. It can also open doors of wonder for them that previous generations could not have even dreamed of. As parents increasingly turn to computers, mobile devices, online games and apps as a means of entertaining their children, it is essential that they don't overlook the important steps to protect them online.

For more information on how you can protect your children from the risks that the online world presents, check out the Kaspersky Lab children's portal: https://kids.kaspersky.com/

5 February 2018

Internet users' online experiences and attitudes

An extract from an Ofcom report.

The complex context for online harm

Everyone uses the internet in their own unique way – making it impossible to generalise about 'typical' internet use

Most participants could not imagine modern life without the internet. Although what they did online varied greatly, their online activities were essential to many aspects of their daily lives and their interactions with others. Most participants were using smartphones to access the internet, even when they owned laptops, tablets or other devices. The internet was often embedded to such an extent that participants did not always recognise they were using the internet, for example by streaming content or playing games.

What participants did online was shaped by their circumstances, personality, and interests, as well as how they felt about using the internet in different ways. Individual experiences were incredibly diverse, with each participant using the internet in their own unique way, mirroring life offline. This variety makes it impossible to generalise about what 'typical' internet use looks like, even among demographic groups.

"Now I don't know what I'd do without it." (Parent, Bristol, household interview)

Despite recognising the benefits, there were common concerns about the online world

Participants identified many important benefits of the internet for them personally, for their family and friends, and for society. For example, middle aged and older participants thought about life back before the internet and emphasised the ease, efficiency and reduced cost of doing things online. Despite these benefits, participants also had strong concerns about the online world. Their worries touched on many different aspects of their lives, and the lives of others, reflecting the extent of their internet use. Participants highlighted worries about harmful conduct (how people treat others online) and harmful content (the types of material that can be accessed online).

Participants found it difficult to know how to protect themselves and their families from harmful conduct in particular

While views about the relative importance of different issues varied, the strongest concerns tended to be about harmful conduct. Participants found it harder to know how to protect themselves and their families from people who want to cause harm to others online. This was often discussed in the context of protecting children and young people but also extended to other vulnerable groups – these are outlined in more detail below.

Hierarchy of concerns about online harm

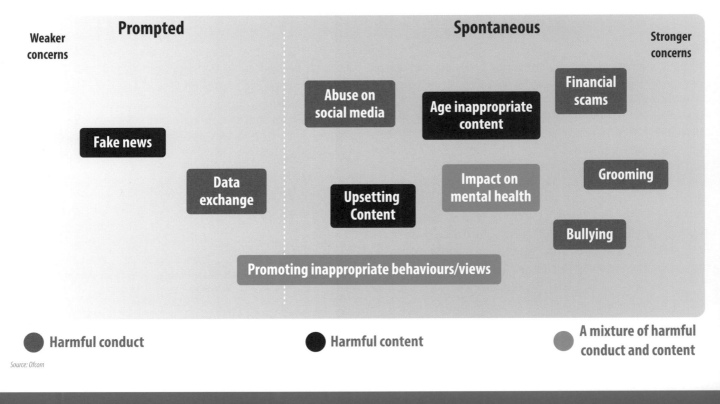

Source: Ofcom

Concerns about harmful content were also widespread and often strong, but these were more familiar to participants. They seemed to understand at least some of the steps they could take to protect themselves and others from potentially harmful content.

Overall, a broad hierarchy of concerns about the online world emerged across the research, summarised. Financial scams (including fraud and misuse of personal data), grooming and bullying were particularly concerning for participants, reflecting the focus on harmful conduct. Participants also worried about the impact of the internet on mental health, and children accessing inappropriate content. The two areas we prompted on (fake news and data exchange) did not emerge as important spontaneous concerns. While participants were worried about these issues after considering them in more detail, overall concerns were not as strong.

Participants focused on older people and children as being at greater risk online, based on perceptions about the harms they might experience

Two demographic groups were considered most at risk online: (i) children and young people, and (ii) older people. For children and young people, participants identified grooming, bullying and age inappropriate content as particular issues. Concerns about older people focused on financial scams and upsetting content. These groups were considered more susceptible to online harms as they were perceived as being:

♦ More likely to be targeted by individuals online with malicious intent;

♦ Less savvy with navigating the online world in different ways;

♦ Less able to make judgements about what is or is not appropriate content and conduct.

Exploring online harm in more detail

Children and young people

Harms to children were a strong, consistent concern

As highlighted above, children and young people were regarded as a potentially vulnerable group online. This was emphasised throughout discussions by both parents and non-parents – although parents were more familiar with specific types of harm and potential protections. In particular, there were strong concerns about children and young people being exposed to general harms online as well as specific harms such as age inappropriate content. Participants felt that this age group might be more susceptible to online harms, for example not having the skills or experience to protect themselves.

"[It] feels like the most worrying are things that harm children because they're not equipped. For me, those are the most concerning." (Gloucester, workshop)

Perceptions of vulnerability differed by age, with younger teenagers seen as the most vulnerable

While experiences varied, many parents described steps they were taking to protect their children online. They were often more confident protecting younger children, describing how they monitored their online activity and used parental locks and filters to control what young children could see. Even so, there were still concerns about children accidentally viewing inappropriate content, or being exposed to harm through under-age access to certain platforms.

Changing protections for children and young people

11 and under (children)
- Parental filters
- Child friendly versions of platforms
- Monitoring accounts e.g. setting up alerts
- Active monitoring e.g. using internet together

12-14 (early teens)
- Conversations about staying safe online
- Checking devices (but recognition they may not be able to see everything)
- Support from siblings

15+ (young adults)
- Keeping profiles private
- Not adding unknown users
- Blocking accounts
- Turning off upsetting content/ scrolling past

Parental protections   Individual protections

Source: Ofcom

Parents often felt they knew the basics of how to keep their children safe, but were unclear on how to navigate the online world as their children got older. This was seen as particularly challenging during the early teenage years, where young people may have (and seek) more independence, have access to their own devices such as smartphones and might be at greater risk of cyber bullying and peer pressure. In this way, this age group was seen as the most vulnerable - stepping away from parental protections but not necessarily having the skills and experience to protect themselves during a vulnerable stage of life.

Parental monitoring decreased in the early teenage years (12-14)

As children entered their teenage years, some parents hoped the skills they had taught them and conversations they had with their children would equip them to navigate the internet as they got older and took on more individual responsibility. They also described how they asked older siblings to monitor their internet use, or asked adult friends to add children on social medial platforms. Although some parents continued to check their teenagers' devices and monitor them online, they lacked confidence in their ability to do this arguing that their children would find a way around protections. Other parents were unsure how they could monitor children at this age, and worried they did not know what their children were doing online.

Young people felt confident online although problems were common

Young people themselves felt confident navigating the internet and responding to harmful content and conduct. Although many described personally seeing upsetting content or experiencing harmful conduct, they did not always see themselves as vulnerable or having experienced "harm". Instead, they often seemed to view this as a feature of the online world. They described putting in place protections such as keeping profiles private, blocking accounts and scrolling past upsetting content. Nevertheless, young people worried about those younger than themselves and what they could be exposed to online.

There was also a recognition that young people may not always feel confident to share their experiences of harm with adults, even if they knew it was the right thing to do. This reflected parents' concerns that they did not know what their children might be exposed to online. This uncertainty led many parents to feel out of control and significantly worried about their children's experiences of the internet.

"I had pretty harassing messages before, it really terrified me for months, I couldn't sleep because of it, and it was just online people trying to mess with me... But I didn't want to tell my parents because I thought oh God what will they think about that." (Glasgow, friendship group)

While parents were seen as responsible for protecting children, they wanted greater support to do this effectively

Parents were seen by adult participants across the board as primarily responsible for looking after their children online. This reflected the role of a parent, as well as the subjective nature of deciding on what is appropriate content for a child. However, participants recognised that there could be more support from platforms and government including greater education to help parents feel confident in doing this. In particular, there was support for age guidance ratings and greater age verification to help parents make decisions about what their children are exposed to. However, there was widespread scepticism about the effectiveness of protections and concerns about the impact greater regulation for children could have on what adults can access online.

"You can't regulate something that the public have access to put stuff onto. Where do you stop? Regulating for children is regulating for us." (Antrim, workshop)

July 2019

Creating a positive online presence

Social media expert Kieran Smyth shares his advice on creating a positive online presence.

Social media has become an integral part of our day-to-day lives. We post if we are happy, sad or even annoyed. Even our evening meal can become a topic of conversation amongst our online connections.

As a generation we tend to put our whole lives out there for the world to see.

Come on, admit it - we've all posted that awful selfie or the angry status update, not to mention the albums full of holiday pics and time spent messing about with our mates.

But what becomes of all these images and tweets?

They become your digital footprint.

What's a digital footprint and why does it matter?

Simply put, your digital footprint is a trail you leave behind on the internet.

If you Googled your name, what would you find? If there's no trace of you, or if what you find is good, then this means you have created a positive online presence.

On the flip side, if you Google your name and you cringe at the results then this means you may have created a negative online presence.

You may ask the question 'so what?' – but have you ever considered what your digital footprint says about you? What would a stranger think if they saw your updates? Imagine if that stranger was a potential employer.

These days employers want to know who they have hired and many recruiters check the social media of potential employees.

Yep, there is a chance that your new boss might turn you down because they don't think that you are a good fit with their company due to how you are portrayed on social media - and it could all come down to one picture.

Kate McKendrick, Recruitment Manager from Hutchison 3G, tells us:

'Before I invite someone for an interview I always make sure to check LinkedIn and Facebook to make sure that the applicant is being truthful and that when they are online they paint themselves in a good light. It is always disappointing when you think you have found an ideal applicant and then their online presence says something completely different about them.

If I do find negative posts online I will make sure to question them about it during the interview process, but on a couple of occasions they have been so bad that I have decided not to interview.'

Top 5 Tips & Tricks

1. Google yourself. It may sound vain but on this occasion you're excused - you need to know what people see when they look for you.

2. If you ain't using it – delete it. Find all of your old profiles and any unused accounts that you no longer use and delete them.

3. Remember, there's more than one page on Google. Make sure to look through as much of Google as you can in case you miss anything

4. Spring clean your history. It will take time but go through your Twitter/Instagram/Facebook and check every post and delete any that paint you in a bad light.

5. Get rid of the evidence. Take down any pictures which make you look bad and ask friends to do the same.

Now what?

Think about what you are posting

You have spent all that time cleaning up your digital footprint. Don't undo all that good work by slipping into old habits and be careful with the content you share.

Go into lock-down

Make sure to tighten up your security settings on platforms like Facebook so that only friends can see you.

Be careful hitting the add button

We all love a new Facebook friend or Twitter follower but be careful. Sometimes it isn't wise to add colleagues or lecturers on social media. It's always a good idea to keep your private life, private.

Create great content

Do things that make you look good and make it a part of your digital footprint. If your boss goes on Facebook, let them find an album of pictures of you volunteering in the community. If you don't already use it – LinkedIn is a great way to showcase all the great stuff you do and can act like an online CV.

Be noticed

Get involved in community activities and get your name mentioned by local newspapers and organisations. It makes you look active, engaged, and more employable online.

Digital skills: how to stay safe online

By Jess Amy Dixon

Do you know what a secure website link looks like? Or what you should do if faced with cyberbullying? Digital skills can help with your career but also your everyday online safety. Find out more.

The internet is an amazing place. It has enabled us to communicate with people all over the world. Many of us now carry pocket-sized devices capable of accessing almost any information we could possibly wish. But life online carries some risks, too. Follow these tips to help you stay legal, responsible, and most importantly safe online.

Protecting your privacy

It's sometimes frightening to think about the level of information which is out there in the world about each of us, thanks to the internet. It's wise to think about what you're putting out there and why. Someone with bad intentions can do an awful lot with a fairly small amount of personal data. Luckily, there are a number of easy steps you can take to boost your protection.

You should consider which sites and services you're using, and if there are more secure alternatives. Google, for example, is ubiquitous but has a pretty terrible privacy record. If you are concerned, try a privacy-focussed browser and search engine such as DuckDuckGo instead. Most browsers have an option called 'private browsing' or similar, which means that temporary internet files ('cookies'), browsing history, form fill data etc. are not saved. Be aware that your internet service provider (and, if you're at work, your employer) will still be able to see which pages you visit, if they are inclined to check. I have known of people who were fired for using work computers or networks inappropriately.

If you use GPS on your mobile device (say, to use it as a Sat Nav,) always turn this off as soon as you are no longer using it. Not only does it drain your battery, having your exact location pinpointed carries serious privacy implications.

Website addresses now usually begin with HTTP or HTTPS. If the site requires any personal data – especially financial data such as credit card information – look for HTTPS and be wary if you do not see it.

It goes without saying that you should always use secure and unique passwords, and never share your login credentials with anyone for any reason. Use a secure password manager such as LastPass to keep all your login details safe.

Social media privacy

Many people now operate two accounts on major social media platforms, one for their 'professional' persona and one for their private life, which may or may not use a pseudonym. Some sites, particularly Facebook, have somewhat cracked down on 'fake' names – but if you use something that plausibly sounds like a real name, you should be fine. A friend of mine uses a name that sounds real (think 'Bob Smith,') but isn't actually his name. Similarly, you can use a false date of birth if you wish, and you shouldn't

put your phone number anywhere online if you can possibly avoid it. I always advocate using two email addresses, one for your work life and one for your private life.

Check your privacy settings. On Twitter, you can 'protect' your tweets (though you may not want to do this if you aim to use your account for professional networking). On Facebook, you can restrict who sees everything from your friends list to your status updates. Always make sure that anything containing personally identifiable information is locked down so only your 'friends' can view it… and be circumspect about who you add as a friend!

Protecting your data & devices

Your data is the info on your computer or phone. It might be photos, contact details, bank details… you name it. Your devices are what you store your info on. Most commonly it will be your personal phone, laptop or desk computer. Sometimes we share computers too… and it's doubly important to make sure your data is protected on a public computer.

Unfortunately, there will always be unscrupulous people trying to gain access to others' data for their own gain. You can never guard completely against any risk, but you should take the following steps to keep your devices – and the data on them – as safe as possible.

Ensure your anti-virus software and firewalls are up to date. These help protect against malicious attacks such as malware, viruses and 'phishng' scams. I like Sophos Home, but you should shop around and pick the right service for you.

Never click a link in an email unless you know the sender. Never, ever respond to such an email with personal or financial information – even if the sender claims to be from your bank, insurance provider or other legitimate organisation. These services will never ask for personal data in this way.

If you're using a public Wi-Fi network, for example in the library or coffee shop, be very careful what information you input as these connections are often not very secure. For anything needing sensitive information, you will be better off waiting until you get home or using your personal mobile data plan.

Secure your mobile device with a screen lock. This can be a pin code or, even more securely, your fingerprint.

Spamming, stalking and hate mail… the ugly world of malicious communications

Did you know it is now a crime in the UK to send 'threatening, abusive or grossly offensive' online communications? Unfortunately it still happens every day.

Never send insulting or threatening messages online. Disagreements happen, particularly if you frequent spaces such as message boards or forums, but there is a huge difference between debating an issue and slinging personal insults. If you find something getting too heated or you feel very angry, step away from the computer and do something else. This is much better than typing something you later regret, and which could have serious consequences.

If someone sends you something threatening or unpleasant, your first line of defence is to report them to the site moderators or owners. Most social media sites will have a 'report' function. Unfortunately these are not always dealt with, or dealt with in a timely manner. You should also block the person responsible.

If harassment continues (such as via the person's friends or through an alternative profile,) you should document everything and consider reporting it to the police.

If you feel frightened or believe there is a credible threat, you absolutely must inform the police immediately.

Web piracy

Just because content is available online does not mean it is free for the taking. Downloading content such as music, TV shows, films and books without permission or payment is piracy – or stealing. People can be and have been prosecuted, resulting in hefty fines and possibly a criminal record. These illegal download services can also result in viruses and malware getting onto your device. Only use legitimate services like Netflix, Spotify, Hulu, Amazon etc. to download media.

Online safety and your physical/mental health

Take care to ensure your computer use isn't affecting your health – mental or physical. If you sit in a desk chair many hours a day, you need to make sure your equipment is appropriate for your needs. Otherwise, you could end up with muscle soreness, eyestrain, headaches, or Repetitive Strain Injury. (I say this as I sit here typing and thinking 'I really need a new desk chair, my back hurts!') A good adjustable chair, a desk of the right height for you, and – if necessary – the right glasses or contact lenses will all minimise your risk.

Remember: if you use computers for work, your employer has a legal obligation to provide any equipment you need to do your job safely.

Psychological health risks can include addiction to certain types of online activity (especially social media), stress from incidents such as cyber-bullying, and poor sleep patterns. Knowing when to stop, taking regular breaks, and not using your device right before bed can all help reduce the impact on your mental health.

There's also growing evidence that the overly filtered and edited world of social media sites like Instagram can contribute to poor body image and dissatisfaction with one's life. This can affect anyone but is particularly prevalent amongst young women. Remember: what people put on social media is highly edited and curated so you see what they want you to see. That perfect selfie isn't what they look like when they roll out of bed. They might be 'hashtag blessed' but they have bad days just like you – I promise.

9 May 2019

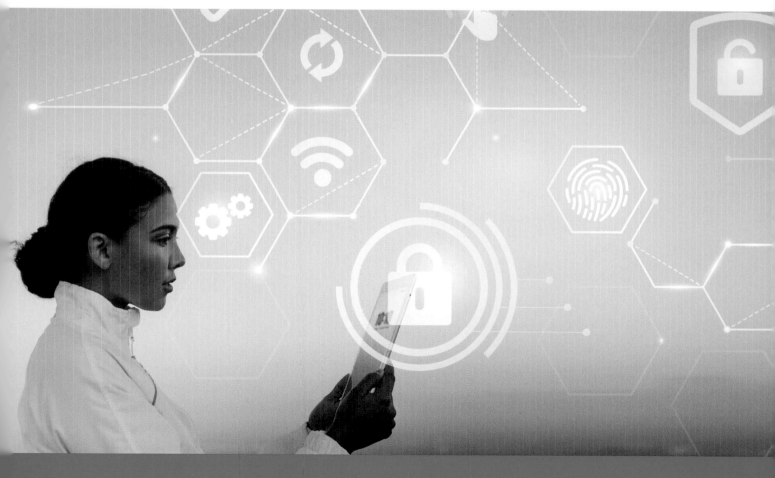

The Internet of Things: how safe are your smart devices?

By Robert Jackman

After years of marketing hype, it seems the much-heralded Internet of Things (or 'IoT' to those in the know) has finally arrived. From washing machines and heating systems that can be controlled from your smartphone, to doorbells that learn to recognise regular visitors and broadcast suspicious activity, more and more of us are upgrading our homes with internet-enabled devices. But have we stopped to think about the cybersecurity of this new technology?

One expert isn't convinced we've thought it through. Mikko Hypponen is chief research officer for the Finnish digital security company F-Secure. Having observed the rise in IoT devices, he's coined a new maxim to alert consumers to their potential dangers: if it's smart, he says, it's also vulnerable. 'It's a pessimistic rule,' he tells me during a stopover in London ahead of an industry speaking gig – 'but it's a true one too: the more connectivity we add to our homes, the more vulnerability we create.'

The big risks for IoT devices fall into two broad categories, he explains – both of which are already being exploited by cyber-criminals. The first and more obvious vulnerability is that smart devices might serve as a backdoor into our home networks, allowing hackers easier access to our laptops and smartphones and all the valuable information (from passwords to credit cards) that entails. In cybersecurity circles, the examples are already becoming legendary: like the Las Vegas casino that reportedly had its high-rollers database stolen by hackers who entered the network via a smart fish-tank.

'Smart devices – like fridges and doorbell cameras – are typically the weakest link in your home network,' Hypponen says. It's a problem compounded by the fact that buyers are rarely encouraged to take even the most basic of safety precautions – such as changing the device's password from its default setting. Along with other new technologies (in particular cryptocurrencies like Bitcoin that allow for untraceable payments) it's led to a spike in ransomware attacks, where hackers render computers useless until the user sends them a large sum of money. One of the most famous ransomware viruses was the Wannacry malware, which infected NHS computers in 2017 – apparently at the instruction of North Korea.

So what can owners do to protect their own devices – and their wider home networks – against attack? One obvious step, according to F-Secure, is to ensure your WiFi network is as secure as possible. That means changing its name (thus making it difficult for hackers to identify its make and model – and, from there, its security flaws), using WPA2 encryption, and ensuring you use a secure password. As for IoT devices themselves, owners should be sure to change the default

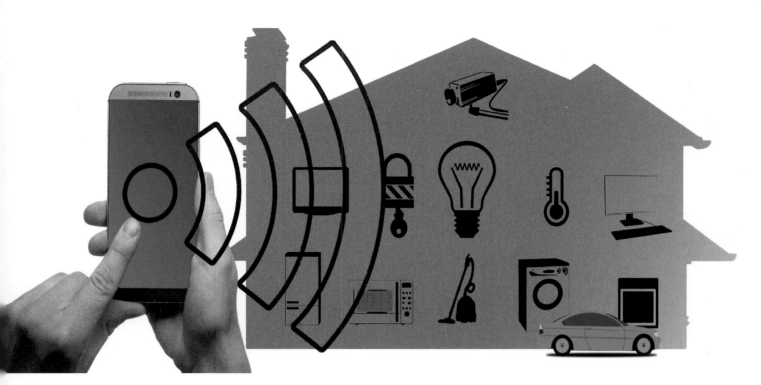

password and also look at disabling certain features – like Universal Plug and Play – which make it easier for hackers to exploit their vulnerabilities.

While ransomware attacks are on the rise, Hypponen is also interested in a newer form of cyber-crime which targets the next wave of smaller IoT devices – like toasters and hairdryers – which connect directly to the internet using 5G. Hang on a minute, I ask. Who needs an internet-enabled toaster? Well, no-one, admits Hypponen. Yet he simultaneously predicts that, as internet-connectivity becomes cheaper and cheaper, it will soon be impossible to buy toasters that don't connect to the internet.

How so? The reason is that toasters aren't going online to provide new functionalities to the customer: instead they'll be providing manufacturers with real-time data on exactly how the device is being used. This kind of mass data is extremely valuable to manufacturers, allowing them to continuously improve their products, but it also makes devices vulnerable to cyber attack – particularly given many use only the most basic encryption and don't always allow users to change their settings. In the past year, Hyponnen says, he's seen more cyber attacks on IoT devices than Windows computers.

Given these devices aren't usually connected to your home network (they access the internet directly through tiny 5G chips), the aim isn't to get hold of your personal data. Hackers want to recruit your devices into their 'botnets' – vast swarms of captive IT addresses that can be used to attack internet servers by sending an overwhelming flood of nonsensical data. In 2016, millions of such devices across the world were harvested in the Mirai botnet, which managed to take down websites from Twitter to the BBC, and Spotify to FoxNews. It remains one of the largest cyber-attacks of recent history.

So what's the solution? Hypponen says that industry has been slow to act – partly because consumers don't suffer directly if their devices are targeted. 'During the Mirai attack, I called one office because we could see that a heat pump in their network was part of the botnet,' he says. 'I asked them "do you own this particular model of pump? Well are you aware it's being used to help take down half of the internet right now?"'. He says that the company was fascinated to hear about the botnet, but weren't particularly motivated to spend their own money to secure their devices. Of course many more won't even know the breach has taken place: a study by the Dutch digital security firm Gemalto found that less than half of businesses were able to identify when an IoT device had been hacked.

Hypponen contrasts the approach taken – by both government and industry – to cybersecurity with the more established approach to consumer safety. 'If you buy a washing machine, you can be certain it's not going to catch fire or give you an electric shock as we certify those things,' he says. 'But there's no regulation at all on whether the machine might end up revealing your WiFi password to hackers.' Though that might be changing: the UK government has begun consulting with experts and industry on how to develop appropriate safeguards, while Finland has just become the first country to introduce a government-backed quality stamp for those products which meet basic cybersecurity standards.

With around a quarter of British homes already using smart devices – and another 40 per cent saying they would consider buying one in the next five years – it's an issue which won't be going away any time soon. Something to keep in mind when you're eyeing up your new toaster.

6 January 2020

Is privacy dead in the age of the internet?

The advent of the internet has given us so many amazing things, but it has also given governments and companies more ways than ever to gather information on people. Data privacy is big news at the moment and a lot of companies like Facebook have come under fire for the way that they are using the data they collect.

Governments are plagued by accusations of election tampering and the general public are beginning to demand more data privacy. The problem is, the technological revolution happened so quickly, legislation was lagging behind and a lot of companies had free rein to do whatever they wanted with your data.

Your average person doesn't always have a full understanding of what data they are giving away and how it is being used, and this has only started to become clear in the last few years.

Governments are beginning to listen to people's concerns about online privacy and there is some legislation in place to protect you online and give you more control over the data that is collected about you. But new technology like voice assistants are bringing up new concerns and there are more fears than ever about the lack of privacy that we have online. The internet is a central part of life and most of us need to use it in some capacity, which means that we don't always have the option of complete privacy. But does that mean that privacy is a thing of the past in the age of the internet?

Some people would say that it is, but that is not an optimistic outlook. The legislation is beginning to catch up and while there is still a long way to go, we are moving in the right direction. The way that we think about data privacy is changing and some prominent politicians, like Andrew Yang, the US Presidential candidate, are arguing that it should be considered a property right. While there are still a lot of people that do not share that view, the tide of opinion is turning. But it could be a long time before attitudes change and the legislation catches up to technology, so what can you do in the meantime? If you are concerned about your data privacy, these are some of the best ways to protect yourself.

Check social media privacy settings

Social media sites are the worst offenders for gathering data about you, but it's not just the data that they collect behind the scenes that you need to worry about. If you are displaying a lot of details about your life on social media, it's easy for anybody to go online and pick up that information because you are offering it up willingly. A quick search for your name will give somebody an insight into your life. If you don't like the idea of that, you need to check your privacy settings. Social media pages are usually set to 'Public' by default, which means that anybody and everybody can view yours. But you can easily change this to private so only people that you are friends with can view them. You could even make it completely private so nobody but you sees them.

As well as changing your privacy settings, you should think carefully about what you put on there. Whenever you are posting, always keep in mind that this information is available online, so think about what you do and don't want to share.

Be careful with public storage

Public storage services like Google Docs are great for backing up files and sharing them easily, but you have to be careful what you put on there. It's important to remember that you are sharing whatever information you put on there with the company that owns the service, and there is always the chance that your account could be hacked. That's why it's never a good idea to store sensitive information on there. For example, if you like to keep a document with all of your passwords on it, don't put that on a public storage service. Keep it saved locally on your computer instead so only you can view it. Any information that you wouldn't share publicly on social media shouldn't be kept on public storage either. Instead, you should get yourself an external hard drive and store things locally, so you have full control over that information.

Wipe old devices

If you throw away an old broken laptop, you probably don't worry about anybody getting at the data on there. But the hard drive is probably still functioning properly and it's not that hard for somebody to gain access to it and take any data that is on there. That's bad news if you have details to do with your bank accounts, for example. That's why it's important to wipe everything completely before throwing it out, just to be safe. But people don't always realize that simply deleting things on your computer doesn't erase them completely, and people can still access that data if they know how. But secure data erasure on NVMe, hard drives and SSDs is simple with WipeDrive, so you need to invest in this specialist software if you want to make sure that your computer has actually been cleared out and nobody can access your data. It's also worth looking into remote wiping, so you can delete your data if your laptop is ever lost or stolen.

Use end-to-end encrypted messages

Most messaging services are encrypted, but people get the wrong idea about what that means. That doesn't mean that your messages are completely protected because they are still decrypted and stored on the server of the provider. That means that somebody could still hack into that server and get access to all of your private messages. If you want to be completely secure, you need to use services that are end-to-end encrypted, like WhatsApp. Facebook messenger does have the capacity for end to end encryption but that is not the default setting, so you will have to enable it manually if you want messages to be truly private.

Review permissions for mobile apps

Your mobile apps collect a lot of data about you and what you are doing on your phone. When you first load up an app, it will usually ask you for permission to access things like the camera, your contacts, and your location. Some apps do actually need access to these things to work properly. For example, any app that involves taking pictures needs to access your camera, but it doesn't need to access your location. A lot of apps ask for these permissions so they can collect data that will be sold on and used for marketing

purposes. It's those ones that you need to watch out for. If an app will not work unless you give it certain permissions, you should consider getting rid of it because it is there to collect your private data and sell it. You should also go into the settings on your phone and check the permissions on all of your apps so you can make sure that you are not giving up data that you shouldn't be.

Avoid public WiFi networks

It's easier than ever to access Wi-Fi when you are out and about. In a lot of cities, there is Wi-Fi access all over, and most coffee shops and restaurants that you go into will have their own Wi-Fi that you can use. But you have to be very careful when using public Wi-Fi networks because it is a big security risk. Most public Wi-Fi networks are not encrypted, which means that it's very easy for hackers to get at your personal information. If you are going to use a public Wi-Fi network, you need to make sure that you are using a VPN. A VPN (virtual private network) gives you an added layer of protection so you are not exposing your personal data when you are on a public Wi-Fi network.

Use strong passwords

This last one is common sense, but most of us are not very good at making strong passwords, even though we know we should be. If you have a weak password, it makes it so much easier for hackers to get into your computer. Using the same password for everything is dangerous as well because once they have cracked one, they can get into all of your accounts. The reason that people use weak passwords is that it's hard to remember a long, complicated password for each one. Ideally, you should be using passwords that are at least 12 characters long and contain numbers and symbols as well as letters. It also needs to be something completely random that doesn't contain things like your name or your birthday because that makes it easier to crack. But remembering those passwords is almost impossible, which is why you should use a password manager instead. It will create different, random passwords for all of your accounts but you only need to remember one single master password. This is the easiest way to make sure that all of your accounts are protected with a strong password.

It's harder than ever to maintain your online privacy and until legislation changes, it's up to you to take steps to protect your own personal information online

10 October 2019

Unreal life: just 22% of Brits believe internet personalities portray life honestly

Most social media users don't trust influencer endorsements – but most engage with them regardless.

By Russell Feldman, Director of Digital, Media and Technology

Brits on social media have major trust issues: two-thirds (66%) believe that people's lives as shown online 'aren't as perfect as they seem'.

But if they're sceptical of people on the whole, they can be especially dubious when it comes to influencers. New research from YouGov reveals that only 22% believe that social media celebrities portray their lives honestly – and just 2% believe they portray their lives in a 'very honest' way.

So how much does this honesty actually matter?

Brits aren't under the influence

A plurality (44%) of Brits say that influencers generally portray their lives dishonestly – and more tellingly, over half (54%) of those who've seen dishonest content from them think it's important for this group to be honest. Just under a quarter (24%) believes authenticity isn't particularly important for online personalities.

In fact, Brits expect more from influencers than they do from their friends and family: only 38% believe it's vital that the people they know are authentic on social media. There may be good reason for this. If Cousin Keith uses a sierra filter to make his holiday photos look a bit better, nobody's really harmed by it; when influencers misrepresent their lives, they can potentially mislead large, young, and impressionable audiences.

Social media users don't trust influencer endorsements...

These impressionable audiences can often be highly valuable for influencers, who can earn money through lucrative partnerships and endorsements.

When asked, 56% of Brits say they haven't seen posts from celebrities/influencers that explicitly plug a company's products or services over the past 30 days – but 18% say they've seen these posts from the people they're following, 13% say they've seen these posts via companies referring to these posts, and 10% say they've seen them through others liking or commenting on them.

Almost half (49%) of those who've seen endorsements from people they follow agree that they're not a genuine representation of the person promoting the product, and 46% think that endorsements aren't believable at all. Only 13% and 16% consider them respectively genuine and believable, with the rest saying they 'don't know'.

...but they pay attention to them anyway

Clearly, there's a real strain of scepticism at work here. But it doesn't necessarily mean that endorsements are useless. For one thing, the same percentage of Brits who don't find endorsements believable also distrust TV ads (46%). Consumers who insist that ads don't work on them might still find that, when it comes down to it, they buy a brand they know from a commercial over a brand they don't know at all. We can apply the same logic to influencer promotions: if most Brits don't trust them, only a quarter (24%) of Brits who've been exposed to this kind of advertisement completely ignore it.

Brits might not always like internet personalities; they might not trust their motives; they might, in some cases, consider them outright dishonest. But they're still paying attention – and attention, positive or otherwise, can be a valuable currency for influencers and the brands who work with them.

31 October 2019

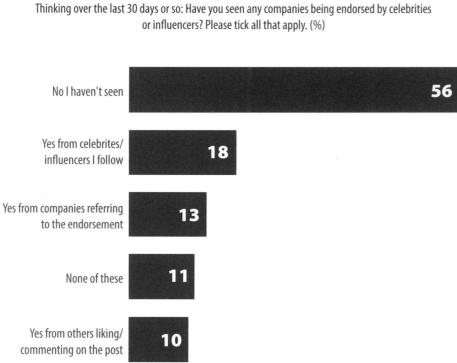

Social media users are seeing indirect influencer endorsements

Thinking over the last 30 days or so: Have you seen any companies being endorsed by celebrities or influencers? Please tick all that apply. (%)

- No I haven't seen: **56**
- Yes from celebrites/influencers I follow: **18**
- Yes from companies referring to the endorsement: **13**
- None of these: **11**
- Yes from others liking/commenting on the post: **10**

Source: YouGov

Youth perspectives on expiring content

An extract from a report from Childnet, a partner in the UK Safer Internet Centre, into children's use and experiences of expiring content.

Expiring content is a key part of many young people's lives. From Snapchat to Instagram stories, expiring content is a way of messaging and sharing photos that many young people use every day. Expiring - or ephemeral - content includes posts, messages and photos that disappear after they have been viewed, or that are only available for a certain amount of time. Children and young people are growing up in a digital world where services such as Facebook, Instagram and Snapchat all have features which allow users to post things that will eventually expire.

This snapshot into how children and young people are using such technology is taken from a poll conducted in February 2019 with over 1,000 young people aged 8-17 in the UK. We also asked the Childnet Digital Leaders to give their thoughts and experiences of expiring content, with 64 responding. The findings give us a clearer picture of how regularly young people use expiring content, what they use it for and how they feel about it.

Key findings

- 7 in 10 young people aged 8-17 have used expiring content in some way over the past year.

- 86% of 13-17's are using expiring content, compared to 62% of 8-12's.

- Over 40% use expiring or disappearing content to message friends every day.

- 65% of young people think it is worth reporting expiring content if it worries or upsets them

Young people's experiences of expiring content

Our research found that 7 in 10 young people in the UK have shared something using expiring content in the last year.

Expiring content is popular among the majority of young people across the 8-17 age range, with 13-17s (86%) more likely to share content using these features than 8-12s (62%). There is no significant difference between girls' (71%) and boys' (75%) use of expiring content.

The most common reason overall for young people to use expiring content is to message friends (67%), with the other reasons being to share something funny (66%) or entertain their friends (64%).

Communicating with friends

67% of 8-17s say they use expiring content to message their friends. Of those:

- 42% say they do this at least once a day.

- Over half (57%) do it at least once a week.

'I like that you can send funny things or tell ur friends what u are doing now but then it disappears' — Secondary pupil

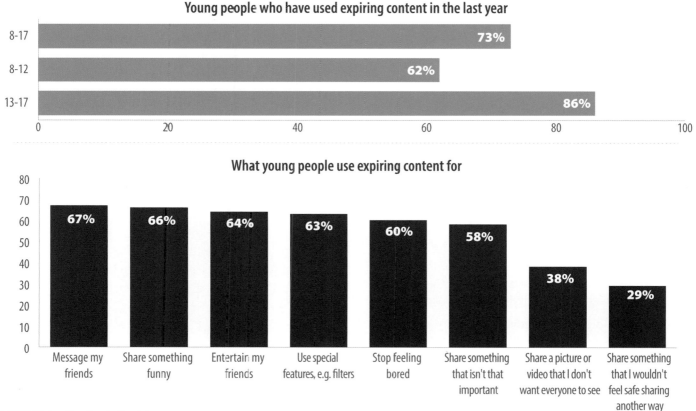

Young people who have used expiring content in the last year

8-17	73%
8-12	62%
13-17	86%

What young people use expiring content for

Message my friends	67%
Share something funny	66%
Entertain my friends	64%
Use special features, e.g. filters	63%
Stop feeling bored	60%
Share something that isn't that important	58%
Share a picture or video that I don't want everyone to see	38%
Share something that I wouldn't feel safe sharing another way	29%

Source: Childnet: Young people's experiences of expiring content

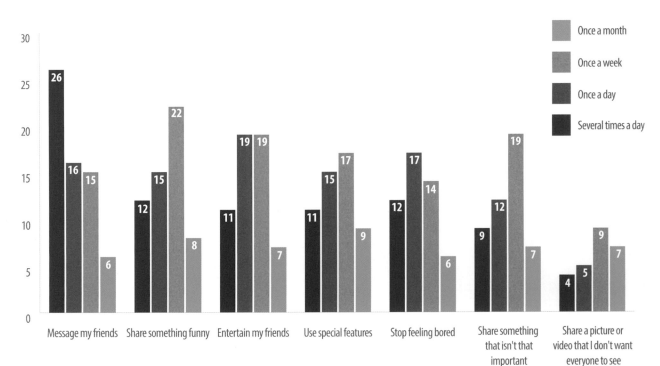

How often do young people use expiring content?

Legend:
- Once a month
- Once a week
- Once a day
- Several times a day

Data (Several times a day, Once a day, Once a week, Once a month):
- Message my friends: 26, 16, 15, 6
- Share something funny: 12, 15, 22, 8
- Entertain my friends: 11, 19, 19, 7
- Use special features: 11, 15, 17, 9
- Stop feeling bored: 12, 17, 14, 6
- Share something that isn't that important: 9, 12, 19, 7
- Share a picture or video that I don't want everyone to see: 4, 5, 9, 7

Source: Childnet: Young people's experiences of expiring content

Two thirds (66%) of respondents aged 8-17 say that they have used the expiring content feature to share something funny.

♦ 27% say they do this on a daily basis.

♦ Teens (13-17s) are more likely to use expiring content to share something funny (81%) than those aged 8-12 (51%).

How young people feel about expiring content

Young people reported their feelings towards expiring content, and the role that it plays in their lives. They use these platforms to interact with their peers, share information and to have fun, as well as to share things they wouldn't want to permanently affect the way they were perceived online.

♦ 41% said they prefer to use expiring content instead of posting something on their profile.

♦ 56% said that people their age use expiring content to share things that they wouldn't normally, because it won't last.

♦ Only 26% said that they can be whoever they want to be when sharing something using expiring content.

Our research found that children and young people are using expiring content to share things that they wouldn't usually on more traditional forms of media.

♦ 38% use it to share a picture or video that they don't want everyone to see, with 9% doing so on a daily basis.

♦ 28% use it to share something that they wouldn't feel safe sharing another way, with some doing this on a daily basis (6%).

When asked why they like using expiring content, many of the Digital Leaders who responded highlighted the practical implications it had for them and their friends.

'It does not clog up space/data on your profile.' Secondary pupil

'People like the idea of it not being there (...) in the future when they are different and may disagree with what they used to post.' Secondary pupil

'If you send a funny picture to your friend it will not be sent to the rest of the world and will stay between your friends.' Secondary pupil

'I like that it limits the amount of time someone can see what I post or send them, it gives me a sense of comfort knowing they can't share it.' Secondary pupil

'(People share) Pictures of themselves, inappropriate pictures e.g nudes, or showing certain parts of their body that they shouldn't. We had a girl at our school who also used this to make racist and mean comments offending certain communities of people.' Secondary pupil

'Send nasty messages thinking it will disappear and nobody will find out. Sending pictures thinking they won't be kept.' Primary pupil

What young people were unsure about, and their concerns

We found that over half of young people who use expiring content are unsure about how it works. Almost half of young people (49%) aren't sure whether content actually disappears completely once it expires. 92% of those surveyed thought that 'posts shared using expiring content don't disappear everywhere'. The young people raised concerns about not knowing what happens to content once it is posted or has expired.

We also found that some young people had confusion around reporting expiring content. 65% of young people thinking it is worth reporting. However many of the Digital Leaders reported not knowing how to report; many giving wrongful explanations of the reporting process.

'They (young people) might choose to use expiring content to share things as it's not there forever (technically it is, though) meaning that only the people who see it first can know what it is.' Secondary pupil

'Many people share a belief that it is purely temporary or their friends wouldn't really take a screenshot of their status or story.' Secondary pupil

'If you send a funny picture to your friend it will not be sent to the rest of the world and will stay between your friends.' Secondary pupil

'No, I don't (know how to report). I know I can take pictures whilst it's up. Apart from that, I would report them as normal.' Secondary pupil

'I'm not quite sure (about reporting) is it in the report button? Maybe screenshot the expiring content?' Secondary pupil

'Young people believe that when the content is gone, it's gone forever.' Secondary pupil

They also cite privacy, how information about them could be given away and storage of the things they post as things that they were unsure of when it came to expiring content.

'Even if it says it expires what really happens to it? Is it deleted or where does it go and who could gain access to it?' Secondary pupil

'What happens to it when it expires? Does the company/app makers see it?' Primary pupil

'Where do our pictures/videos go when they expire? Where is the data/information stored?' Primary pupil

5 tips from Childnet Digital Leaders on using expiring content

#1 Be positive

"Use it in a good way... like wishing someone a happy birthday"

"Say nice things, don't be rude"

"Post things which will benefit yourself and others and use your platform to spread positivity"

#2 Remember screenshots of expiring content can be taken

'Be careful of what you send or say because someone could screenshot it.'

'They may disappear but people may have screenshotted your post so don't write anything you would not want someone to see'

'Be careful what you post, because even if it is non- lasting, it could potentially contribute to your digital footprint in the future'

#3 Don't post personal information

'Avoid posts that clearly show your whereabouts or your school'

'Don't post anything that will reveal personal information'

#4 Think about what you are posting

'Don't put up anything embarrassing or hurtful'
'Don't publish silly/dangerous things for others to see'

#5 Know how and when to report hurtful or harmful posts

'When you see something wrong report it'

Source: Childnet: Young people's experiences of expiring content

The above information is reprinted with kind permission from Childnet.
© 2020 Childnet International

www.childnet.com

One in four teenagers have received a 'sext' by the age of 18, study claims

One in seven teens are actively sending 'sexts'.

By Olivia Petter

'Sexting' is the colloquial portmanteau attributed to the exchange of digital messages containing sexually explicit material in the form of text or imagery - and it's rife amongst teens, a new study has found.

While one in seven teenagers have sent sexts, the study of more than 110,000 teens around the world revealed that one in four have received them.

Researchers attribute this rise to the ubiquity of smartphones, as this is where the large majority of participants conduct their sexting activities rather than on the computer.

Conducted at the University of Calgary, the team of psychology professors concluded that sexting was a normal part of the teenage experience.

However, in today's hyper-digital climate it's all too easy for this kind of explicit communication to go entirely unregulated, putting young people at risk of exploitation.

Not to mention the myriad emotional consequences, from humiliation and objectification to utter hopelessness and social isolation, there's no telling what may happen if a sext spirals out of control.

'Smartphones give easy access to this sort of behaviour, and more people are acquiring them,' explains dating psychologist Madeleine Mason.

'Thus, it's never been easier for young people to access and create sexual content online,' she added.

Cause for concern was highlighted in the research when they uncovered the number of teens who admitted to forwarding on sexts without consent from the original sender.

The research, which involved a literature review of more than 39 studies of children between the ages of 12 and 17, revealed that one in 10 teens have sent sexts in this unsolicited manner.

Naturally, this has sparked concerns regarding the number of naked images or sexual messages that could be circulating amongst teens without the sender's knowledge, something the study uncovered as having happened to 8.4 per cent of teens.

'An important area of future inquiry will be the identification of variables associated with non-consensual sexting, as well as the evaluation of the effectiveness of educational campaigns and legal policies striving to mitigate non-consensual sexting in youth,' the researchers wrote.

Difficulties can emerge when it comes to defining 'sexting' in legal terms, explains Olliers solicitor Zita Spencer.

'Any text message with sexual content could be considered a 'sext' e.g. sexually suggestive or explicit wording, images of a sexual nature or of nudity,' she told The Independent.

'This is a growing problem within school age children. Social media and apps such as WhatsApp and Snapchat make the sending of messages/images amongst groups easier and cheaper.'

Spencer added that while the legal age of consent for sex is 16, it is illegal to make an indecent image of anyone under 18.

'Many children are not aware that their 'sexting' activities constitute a criminal offence or the risks they are exposing themselves to,' she said.

The NSPCC outlines the risks of sexting on their website, explaining that a young person is breaking the law if they take an explicit photo or video of themselves or a friend.

'It is an offence to take, possess and share indecent images of those under the age of 18 - and this offence can be committed by young people,' explains Dr Samantha Pegg, senior lecturer at Nottingham Law School.

'So where sexts include indecent images of children, all the parties involved, from those taking and sharing images to those in possession, may be committing offences,' she told The Independent.

'This is true even if those images have been created or shared consensually,' she added.

So, even if someone under the age of 18 has sent an indecent image of themselves, they are committing an offence by distributing it to anyone else, who would then be in possession of an indecent image of a child which is, in turn, a criminal offence.

27 February 2018

Children under the age of 14 are being arrested for 'sexting' in police postcode lottery

Exclusive: Data shared with i reveals huge inconsistency in the application of guidance designed to stop children being criminalised.

By Will Hazell

Teenagers are still being criminalised for 'sexting' despite police guidance designed to stop young people ending up with a criminal record, i can reveal.

Analysis of police data by academics from the University of Suffolk - shared with i - shows there is a 'postcode lottery' in how police forces deal with sexting, with children under the age of 14 continuing to be arrested.

Under the 1978 Protection of Children Act, the generation or distribution of indecent images of children is illegal.

However, the legislation could not have predicted the rise in young people sending indecent photos of themselves to peers with the advent of smartphones.

To address the increasing number of children being arrested for sexting, in December 2016 the College of Policing introduced new guidance, known as 'Outcome 21'.

An Outcome 21 means a crime is recorded but taking action against the minor is judged 'not in the public interest', and they do not get a criminal record.

However, figures obtained under Freedom of Information show huge inconsistency in how it is being applied.

While the data cannot reveal the complexity of each case, it shows that since December 2016 some forces have made great use of Outcome 21.

Police inconsistency

For example, Staffordshire Police utilised Outcome 21 on 659 occasions while making just five arrests of under-18s.

But in Hampshire arrests of under-18s far outweighed the use of Outcome 21. Over the same period Hampshire Constabulary arrested 16 young people aged 17 or under, including one aged younger than 14, while issuing just two Outcome 21s.

A spokesman for Hampshire Constabulary said: 'As a force we assess each report received on a case-by-case basis.

'Where possible, we always try not to criminalise children unless it is in the public interest and we have a wide variety of options available to us.

'There are over 20 different types of response we can use and our officers carefully consider each individual case before making a decision.

'We also have a scrutiny panel, which meets monthly, to ensure our use of Outcome 21 is appropriate.'

The FOI request, which was responded to by 31 police forces in England and Wales, shows that since December 2016 38 children under the age of 14 have been arrested across 10

forces in relation to making or distributing an indecent image.

In total there were 358 arrests of minors over the period. While Ministry of Justice data on convictions is not yet available for 2018, 54 minors were proceeded against for these crimes in 2017 and 38 convicted.

Tink Palmer, chief executive of the Marie Collins Foundation - a charity which works with child victims of image-based abuse and commissioned the research - said she was 'pleased that a number of progressive police forces are using Outcome 21'.

However, she added: 'In some areas children are still being arrested and subject to the full law enforcement process and a criminal record instead of Outcome 21 being applied. There is a risk that children engaging in sexting are falling victim to a postcode lottery.

'I would like to see the guidance being applied every time it is appropriate to do so and applied in the same way by all police forces across the country, whilst, at the same time, we continue educating children about the risks of engaging in this kind of activity.'

Professor Andy Phippen - co-author of the analysis with Professor Emma Bond - told i that while Outcome 21 is a step forward, he is still concerned that 'in some forces they're being given out like sweeties'.

'Emotional trauma'

He pointed out that an Outcome 21 report may still 'come back to haunt you', because it can appear on a criminal record check at the discretion of a Chief Constable.

He described the current law as 'a mess', and urged police officers to use their discretion where appropriate by giving advice to young people rather than automatically recording a crime.

Professor Phippen said schools and the police had to be more sensitive in dealing with sexting. He gave one example where a girl in her early teens was summoned to the headteacher's office at her school, where the head, the police and her parents 'went through her images on her phone with her'.

'The emotional trauma of that must have been somewhat significant,' he added.

6 December 2019

Online gaming: tips for playing safe

There's a game out there for everyone. Some might prefer sporting games like FIFA and NBA. Others play adventure games such as Fortnite and Minecraft. Video games are arguably better than ever - because almost all of them allow you to play online with friends.

It's not just young people that are gaming online. Did you know that there are over 2 billion gamers across the world? (Newzoo, Global Games Market Report, 2018). And these gamers aren't just wasting their time - the benefits of gaming include improvement of coordination, problem-solving skills and brain speed to name a few.

Gaming is more fun when people...

♦ Treat others with respect

♦ Play fairly and within the rules of the game

♦ Keep personal information private

♦ Make sure that content they're sharing is not racially, religiously or sexually offensive

Chatting to other gamers can make it more fun too. It's likely that you'll chat to people that you've never met in real life. They might make you laugh, or give you great gaming tips. And it can feel like you know them well, especially if you voice chat with them through an app like Discord. But remember - it's easy for people to lie online, and some gamers might put pressure on you to do things you're not comfortable with.

Listen to yourself

People online sometimes ask us to do things that we don't want to do. Listen to yourself and trust your gut instincts before taking the next step.

Gamers to look out for

They seem too good to be true

Do they like all the same things as you? Do they say nice things about you all of the time? It's great to game with people that you have things in common with, but sometimes people lie to build a relationship with you, and pressure you into doing things.

They want to chat in private

Nearly all games have the option to 'chat' - you don't need to add gamer friends on private messaging apps like Skype or WhatsApp anymore. Avoid private chats as people are more likely to make you uncomfortable there.

They say sexual things

If they try to talk to you about sex, and particularly if they want to talk about sex quickly, they're probably not a 'real' friend. If their sexual chat makes you feel uncomfortable, you could speak to an adult that you know and trust (like a teacher).

They're much older than you

Gamers come in all different shapes and sizes. You're likely to have fun chatting with gamers of all ages. But it's strange for adults to try and get really close to you, read our advice about dealing with older 'friends'.

They put pressure on you

It's never ok for someone to make you feel like you have to do something. Good friends don't tell you what to do, or who you can and can't be friends with. If someone has pressured or forced you to take a naked pic, it is never too late to get help, report to CEOP.

5 steps for safer gaming

Block people that make you feel uncomfortable

If someone makes you feel upset, block them so they can't make you feel that way again.

Keep personal information private

Don't give out any personal information that could identify you or your location. Rather than using a photo of yourself as your profile picture, why not create an avatar to use instead?

Be careful about meeting up

It's always best not to meet up with people that you only know online. Even if you have mutual friends, they could still be lying about who they are. If you do decide to meet up, take a trusted adult with you. And always meet in a busy public place.

Take breaks

When you're spending a lot of time on a game, it can be difficult to tell if your gamer friends are real or not. Take regular breaks and talk to family and friends about your gaming world.

Speak to a trusted adult

If anyone makes you feel uncomfortable, talking to someone about what's happened might make you feel better. Perhaps there's an adult that you know and trust that you could talk to. Or you could speak to a counsellor at Childline confidentially by calling 0800 1111.

Blocking and reporting in games

Most games (whether they're played on a PC, games console or mobile app) will allow you to block and report users that upset you. This is done in slightly different ways on every game and/or platform. Usually you find a player's profile, or their name in your friends list, and then click block/report.

Blocking

When you block someone it normally means that although they can still send you messages, you will not receive them.

Reporting

Sometimes blocking isn't enough. Some users should be reported to stop them from contacting other gamers too. Report users that:

♦ Stalk, bully, discriminate against or abuse you or other users

♦ Are disruptive or threatening

♦ Share other users' and your own personal and account information.

Are you being bullied in an online game?

If you're being bullied, there's lots of help and advice out there.

Talk to Childline

On the Childline site you can find out more about online bullying. Being bullied can really knock your confidence so they also provide tips on ways to be assertive which can help deal with bullying and build up your self-esteem.

You can also speak to a counsellor on 0800 1111.

www.childline.org.uk

www.thinkuknow.co.uk

Key Facts

- 87% of all adults used the internet daily or almost every day in 2019. (page 1)

- Over 8 out of 10 adults accessed the internet 'on the go' in 2019. (page 1)

- Email was used by 86% of adults in 2019, more than any other internet activity. (page 2)

- The percentage of adults making voice or video calls using the internet more than trebled over the past decade, rising from 16% in 2009, to 50% in 2019. (page 2)

- 83% of internet users now pay their bills online, up from 59% in 2013. (page 4)

- Among non-internet users 69% cite 'lack of interest' as the main reason for not being online, down from 82% in 2013. (page 4)

- A survey has revealed UK adults spend around 50 days a year on their mobiles. (page 5)

- The top five screen time activities revealed in a UK survey included messaging friends & family (67%), browsing social media (59%), reading the news (48%), watching & listening to music (49%) and online shopping (35%). (page 5)

- In April 2019, the World Health Organization (WHO) recommended children aged between two and five years old should not exceed one hour of screen time daily. (page 7)

- Half of 12-15s who go online had seen hateful content in the last year, up from a third in 2016. (page 10)

- 18% of 12-15 year olds use social media to support causes and organisations by sharing or commenting on posts, up from 12% in 2018. (page 10)

- Almost half of girls aged five to 15 now play games online – up from 39% in 2018. The proportion of boy gamers is unchanged at 71%, but boys spend twice as long playing online each week as girls. (page 10)

- 50% of 10 year-olds own a smartphone in 2019, up from 30% in 2015. (page 11)

- Posting online material inciting hatred and violence on the grounds of race, religion or sexual orientation is criminalised under the Public Order Act 1986. (page 15)

- Results from a new survey by Kaspersky Lab show that a huge 87 per cent of parents admit that they don't restrict how much time their young children spend online. (page 20)

- According to Internetsafety101.org, 90 percent of teens who participate in social media have ignored bullying that they've witnessed online, and one third have been victims of cyber-bullying themselves. (page 20)

- An Ofcom report identified two demographic groups who were considered most at risk online: (i) children and young people, and (ii) older people. For children and young people, participants identified grooming, bullying and age inappropriate content as particular issues. Concerns about older people focused on financial scams and upsetting content. (page 23)

- An Ofcom report found parental monitoring of devices and online activity decreased in the early teenage years (ages 12-14). (page 24)

- Cryptocurrencies like Bitcoin that allow for untraceable payments have led to a spike in ransomware attacks, where hackers render computers useless until the user sends them a large sum of money. One of the most famous ransomware viruses was the Wannacry malware, which infected NHS computers in 2017 – apparently at the instruction of North Korea. (page 28)

- A lot of apps ask for permissions such as access to camera, contacts and location so they can collect data that will be sold on and used for marketing. Some apps do actually need access to these things to work properly. For example, any app that involves taking pictures needs to access your camera, but it doesn't need to access your location. If an app will not work unless you give it certain permissions you should consider getting rid of it because it is there to collect your private data and sell it. (page 31)

- Most public Wi-Fi networks are not encrypted, which means that it's very easy for hackers to get at your personal information. (page 31)

- Two-thirds (66%) of Brits on social media believe that people's lives as shown online 'aren't as perfect as they seem'. (page 32)

- From Snapchat to Instagram stories, expiring content is a way of messaging and sharing photos that many young people use every day. Expiring – or ephemeral – content includes posts, messages and photos that disappear after they have been viewed, or that are only available for a certain amount of time. (page 33)

- The most common reason overall for young people to use expiring content is to message friends (67%), with the other reasons being to share something funny (66%) or entertain their friends (64%). (page 33)

- 56% (of young people) said that people their age use expiring content to share things that they wouldn't normally, because it won't last. (page 34)

- While one in seven teenagers have sent sexts, a study of more than 110,000 teens around the world revealed that one in four have received them. (page 36)

- Under the 1978 Protection of Children Act, the generation or distribution of indecent images of children is illegal. (page 37)

Broadband Internet Access

Usually shortened to just broadband, this refers to the telecommunications signal which is of greater bandwidth than the standard/usual signal. The broader the band, the greater the capacity for traffic which means faster download speeds.

Child Sexual Exploitation (CSE)

Using or exploiting a child for sexual purposes. This often goes hand-in-hand with the grooming process and can involve offering the child money, gifts, cigarettes or alcohol in return for sexual favours. CSE can lead to child trafficking and prostitution.

Cybercrime

Crime with some kind of computer or cyber aspect to it: using modern telecommunication networks such as the Internet (like chat rooms, e-mails and forums) and mobile phones (texting) to intentionally psychically or mentally harm and cause distress. Computer viruses, cyberstalking, identity theft and phishing scams are some examples of cybercrime.

Digital footprint

The 'trail' a person leaves behind when they interact with the digital environment. This evidence left behind gives clues as to the person's existence, presence and identity. It also refers to what other people may say about you online, not just yourself: sometimes also referred to as your online presence.

Digital literacy

The ability to think critically about information consumed online, to be able to use the internet safely and with proficiency.

Digital native

A person who has grown up surrounded by digital technology, such as mobile phones, computers and the Internet (the current 12 to 18-year-old generation).

E-commerce

Electronic business transactions, usually occurring via the Internet, e.g. purchasing goods online.

General Data Protection Regulation (GDPR)

A law that enables EU citizens to have control over their personal data and how it is used. GDPR places legal obligations on companies and organisations to maintain and protect our personal data. The legislation came into force across the European Union on 25 May 2018.

Grooming

Actions that are deliberately performed in order to encourage a child to engage in sexual activity. For example, offering friendship and establishing an emotional connection, buying gifts, etc.

In-app purchasing

This refers to purchases made 'within' an app. For example, if you download a free app and are then asked to buy 'upgrades' that allow you more lives or access to different parts of the game. Often, children make accidental purchases through their parents' accounts when devices remember passwords and account information.

Internet

A worldwide system of interlinked computers, all communicating with each other via phone lines, satellite links, wireless networks and cable systems.

Internet of Things

This term refers to the network of objects that now connect via the Internet. For example, cars, watches, fridges, etc.

Internet Watch Foundation

A charity that works to minimise the availability of child abuse images and other criminal adult content on the Internet.

Online harms

Content or activity that can cause harm to internet users, particularly children and vulnerable people. These behaviours can harm people either emotionally, or physically

Phishing

Phishing is when someone fraudulently sends emails with the intent to gain your personal information, such as passwords and bank details. The emails are usually made to look like they are from reputable companies, but they link to a fraudulent website to trick people into entering sensitive information.

Screen time

A term used to refer to the amount of time someone (usually young children) spends in front of a screen. For example, a tablet, smartphone or computer.

Sexting

Someone uploading and sending an indecent, usually sexually graphic, image to their friend or boy/girlfriend via mobile phone or the Internet.

Smartphone

A mobile device with advanced capabilities, much like a handheld computer. One popular example is the Apple iPhone. They are increasingly being used to access the Internet and may have other features such as a camera, GPS and MP3 player.

Social media

Media which are designed specifically for electronic communication. `Social networking' websites allow users to interact using instant messaging, share information, photos and videos and ultimately create an online community. Examples include Facebook, LinkedIn and micro-blogging site Twitter.

Activities

Brainstorming

♦ In small groups, discuss what you know about the Internet of Things.

- What does the term 'Internet of Things' refer to?
- What kinds of things are included in this definition?
- How many things in your classroom use the internet?

♦ In small groups, discuss what you know about online safety and online harms.

- What is online safety?
- Make a list of things that you can do to stay safe online.
- What should you do if you see something upsetting online?

Research

♦ Talk to a relative who is older than you. Find out how technology has changed since they were your age. Ask about their first experiences of using the Internet. Make some notes and create a presentation to share with your class.

♦ Look at some of the statistics from the article 'UK's screen time stats revealed'. Use these as a starting point to create your own questionnaire or survey about Internet usage in your class and create a graph from the results. You can ask people what kind of activities they do online and how much time they spend on the computer.

♦ In small groups, research some charities and organisations that people can go to for help and advice if they have experienced any online harms.

♦ Lots of social media platforms have a minimum age requirement. Choose three and research their minimum age. Do you think this is suitable? What have they done to protect younger users?

♦ Choose one of your favourite social media sites and research how to report upsetting content or cyberbullying. Do they have a clear guide on how to report someone? Do they make it easy to report, or is it difficult? Make notes on your findings.

Design

♦ Create a 'how-to' guide for an older person who has just bought a smartphone. Introduce them to some apps you think they might find useful, and explain how they work.

♦ Choose one of the articles from this topic and create an illustration that highlights the key themes of the piece.

♦ Create a campaign to raise awareness of internet dangers. Use the article 'The ten internet dangers to kids – and how you can stop them' to help you.

♦ Design a leaflet on online safety. Include tips and signpost where people can go for help if something they have experienced online has upset them.

♦ Create a Digital Literacy poster for your school. How important is it for children to be digitally literate? Do you think it should be taught as part of the school curriculum?

♦ Design a poster highlighting the dangers of Internet addiction. Be sure to include information about clear symptoms and the effects of Internet addition.

♦ Design a leaflet on Phishing. Include things to look out for when getting emails from companies, how to report fake emails, and what to do if you think you have been scammed.

♦ Choose one of the articles in this book and create an infographic to display the information in that article.

Oral

♦ 'Is the internet good or bad?' Divide your class in half and debate this question, with half arguing in favour and half arguing against.

♦ In pairs, discuss what you think the age of consent for social media platforms like Facebook and Twitter should be. Feedback to your class.

♦ What impact has the Internet had on people's privacy? Discuss in pairs.

♦ In small groups, think about some of the difficulties older people might experience in a more internet-based future. List some things they might struggle with. For example, online banking or social media.

♦ How do you think parents can protect their children online? Discuss this with a partner.

♦ 'Is privacy dead in the age of the internet?', In small groups, discuss this and make notes on your ideas.

♦ In pairs, one be the parent, and one the child. Role-play the discussion that they might have about staying safe online. Who knows more, the parent or the child?

Reading/writing

♦ Do you think that young adult literature accurately reflects the reality of the way teens use social media? Are there any books that you know of that feature social media as part of the plot? If you are not sure, ask your librarian or friends for recommendations.

♦ Imagine you are an Agony Aunt/Uncle and that someone has written to you with fears that their son/daughter is addicted to using their smartphone. Write a helpful reply.

♦ What would the world be like without the Internet? In groups, discuss this statement and then produce a presentation about your discussion results. How would communication differ? What kind of impact would it have on bullying? What about shopping?

♦ Choose one of the articles in this book and write a short one-paragraph summary. Choose five key points and list them.

♦ Write a persuasive letter to your headteacher on the benefits of allowing students to use their phones in class.

Acknowledgements

The publisher is grateful for permission to reproduce the material in this book. While every care has been taken to trace and acknowledge copyright, the publisher tenders its apology for any accidental infringement or where copyright has proved untraceable. The publisher would be pleased to come to a suitable arrangement in any such case with the rightful owner.

The material reproduced in ISSUES books is provided as an educational resource only. The views, opinions and information contained within reprinted material in ISSUES books do not necessarily represent those of Independence Educational Publishers and its employees.

Images

Cover image courtesy of iStock. All other images courtesy of Pixabay and Unsplash, except pages 36: Freepik, 27 & 30: Rawpixel

Icons

Icons on page 10 were made by PixelPerfect and Freepik from www.flaticon.com.

Illustrations

Don Hatcher: pages 12 & 24. Simon Kneebone: pages 21 & 39. Angelo Madrid: pages 3 & 28.

Additional acknowledgements

With thanks to the Independence team: Shelley Baldry, Danielle Lobban, Jackie Staines and Jan Sunderland.

Tracy Biram

Cambridge, May 2020